SIR ROBERT HUNTER'S DRAMATIC WALKS

Hindhead Common
and
Waggoners Wells

Cover illustrations –
Front: The Cross on Gibbet Hill
in morning sunlight, October 2010
Back: Waggoners Wells, October 2020
'Highwayman' on Hindhead, May 2013
'Sir Robert' addressing the walkers, August 2010

Sketch of Sir Robert Hunter (1844–1913), co-founder of The National Trust and resident of Haslemere attired for walking

SIR ROBERT HUNTER'S DRAMATIC WALKS

Walk in the footsteps of Sir Robert Hunter

co-founder of The National Trust

over
Hindhead Common
and
Waggoners Wells

———

Plus a short history
of The National Trust's acquisitions
at the west of The Weald

———

John Owen Smith

Sir Robert Hunter's Dramatic Walks

Published 2023

Replaces:
The Sir Robert Hunter Trail ISBN 1-873855-13-3
and *Hindhead is Safe* ISBN 978-1-873855-61-4

Typeset and published by John Owen Smith
19 Kay Crescent, Headley Down, Hampshire GU35 8AH

Tel: 01428 712892
wordsmith@johnowensmith.co.uk
www.johnowensmith.co.uk

© John Owen Smith 1994, 2010, 2015, 2023

The right of John Owen Smith to be identified as the author of this work has been asserted by him in accordance with the Copyright, Designs and Patents Act 1988.

All rights reserved. No part of this publication may be reproduced by any means, electronic or mechanical, including photocopy or any information storage and retrieval system without permission in writing from the publisher.

ISBN 978-1-873855-79-9

Printed by KDP

Contents

Introduction	7
How the National Trust obtained Hindhead Common	
Biographies *of people mentioned in the book*	25
Calendar of Events	33
Dramatic Walks	39
Over Hindhead Common	41
Around Waggoners Wells	65

View over the Devil's Punch Bowl in 1938

Introduction

How the National Trust obtained Hindhead Common

*The 'Balance of Trust' as illustrated by Thelma Ede
for the National Trust Centenary in 1995*

'HINDHEAD IS SAFE'

Background

It is strange how the same place can affect different people in completely different ways. To William Cobbett on his *Rural Ride* of November 1822, Hindhead was "that miserable hill, the most villainous spot that God ever made," which he "distainfully scorned to go over." Yet to John Tyndall in the 1880s, it was "the Switzerland of England" with air as pure as that in the Alps, and the place where he chose to build a "retreat for his old age."

Until recently, many modern drivers agreed with Cobbett, and sought alternative routes around the congestion at the A3 Hindhead crossroads – some perhaps making their way through the side-roads which Cobbett failed to find all those years ago. Others, less rushed, who found time to stop and explore the heaths and tracks in the area, were more inclined to Tyndall's view.

The road from London to Portsmouth then climbed up the northern spur of Hindhead and at one time ran virtually to the summit, where it turned sharply west. At a junction there another road led down into Haslemere. The way was improved in 1826 by a new cutting made lower down in the Punch Bowl, and it was this route which the A3 trunk road used. The older route became in effect a bridleway, and the track from the summit down to Haslemere was no longer used, although it can still be followed today and eventually becomes Farnham Lane.

At 272 metres (892 ft) above sea level, the summit at Hindhead is known as Gibbet Hill. It commands views over many miles, especially to north and east, and on a clear day it rivals that from neighbouring Blackdown, which Tennyson described as "green Sussex fading into blue, with one grey glimpse of sea."

Surrounded by many hundreds of acres of unspoilt heathland, including the Devil's Punch Bowl, the place can seem idyllic on a warm summer's day. But it was not always so.

The name 'Gibbet' gives a clue to the darker side of its history, for this was indeed the spot where criminals were hanged and their tarred bodies left to swing in clanking irons until they rotted. These were the three men executed here in 1787 for murdering an anonymous sailor, whose story is told on the nearby *Sailor's Stone* and whose body now rests in Thursley churchyard.

Introduction

A sketch made of Hindhead by the artist Turner in 1807 clearly shows the gibbet on the summit, and the wooden upright was apparently still standing here in 1827. Not surprisingly, the place got a reputation for being haunted, and in 1851 Sir William Erle had the present granite Cross erected on the site to try to dispel these fears. Around its base runs a Latin inscription which translated reads: *"After the darkness, light; In death, peace; In light, hope; After death, salvation."*

Turner's sketch of Hindhead

Shortly afterwards, in January 1859, the railway arrived at Haslemere offering an alternative, safer and faster route from London to Portsmouth. It also opened up the area around Haslemere as a commuter belt. Some would say this shook a bit of life into a region which had sunk into lethargy since the first Reform Bill disenfranchised it in 1832; others that it marked the end of the old village of Haslemere and the start of an inevitable progression towards urban sprawl.

Enclosures and Exclusions

Before the building of the railway, other changes had occurred around Haslemere which added significantly to the effect of its arrival. Chief among these were the considerable enclosures of neighbouring common land.

G.R. Rolston in his book *Haslemere* tells us that until the mid-19th century all the country from Shottermill to Farnham was "heathy common land" and much of it was contained in the old Woolmer Forest. The roads to Farnham over this waste were said to be so bad that anyone who valued his carriage springs drove via Milford and Elstead. By means of the enclosures, some seven to eight thousand acres of common land were lost to the public. Much of the money received in payment of these lands was allotted to the making of new roads.

Enclosure Acts tended to be raised on a parish by parish basis, and while they were made for the parishes of Frensham and Headley (and Grayshott was in Headley parish at the time), the parish of Witley was left unchanged – so most of the Devil's Punch Bowl and Hindhead Common were spared the results.

Introduction

But in enclosed parishes, the local population of broomsquires and others who had from time immemorial made their living off the 'wastes of the manor' were excluded from their traditional resources. The land was parcelled up and sold to rich 'incomers', who usually fenced it off and denied them access. At one and the same time then, there arrived both the means of ready access from London and elsewhere, and the incentive for outsiders to come along and buy the recently enclosed plots to build country homes. In short, the area was earmarked for invasion.

The Railway Arrives

From the late 1830s the railway network had been extending from London into Surrey, reaching Woking in 1838, Guildford in 1845, and Godalming in 1849. From there, plans were drawn up for a link through to Portsmouth via Haslemere and Petersfield, which was indeed completed in 1859. Four years earlier, Haslemere had been the scene of a tragedy in which, for the first time, a Surrey police officer was killed on duty.

The 'navvies' who built the railways were generally a hard-living, hard-drinking bunch, putting fear into the communities through which the lines were being pushed, and more particularly when they descended on the town's pubs to spend their pay packets on drink. On the night of Saturday 28th July 1855, the entire Haslemere police force of just two men was occupied enforcing the midnight closing time in and around the High Street. They had particular trouble with a group of five 'navvies' at the *King's Arms* (then next to the *White Horse*), one of whom accused Inspector Donaldson of laying a hand on him at the bar. The argument continued outside, in the Market Place, when Constable Freestone stepped in to protect his superior and pushed the protester to the ground.

One thing led to another, and the man, Thomas Woods, eventually returned holding a large iron bolt and hit Donaldson over the head with it. Others kicked him as he lay on the ground before they finally dispersed. The Inspector was helped home, but lapsed into a coma and died during the night. Woods was arrested and sentenced to 20 years transportation on a charge of unpremeditated manslaughter; his four colleagues were given lesser sentences of 2 to 6 years hard labour.

Once the traumas of actually building the railway had faded in their minds, however, the people of Haslemere would have started to get used to having this new form of transport available to them.

Introduction

Fares to London in 1864 were about 6/- second class or 8/- first class, with five trains in each direction on weekdays and two on Sundays. The fastest scheduled journey time was 1 hour 19 minutes between Haslemere and Waterloo, and the last trains of the day departed from both London and Portsmouth at about 7 pm.

It seems that, at least until the turn of the century, one could also charter a train to run outside these hours. Flora Thompson in her book *Heatherley* mentions a rich lady living near Grayshott who ordered a night telegraph service to be arranged so that her London specialist might be summoned by special train from Waterloo if her 'interesting event' arrived during the night. As it turned out the arrangement was not needed as the child made its appearance at a time when trains were running normally.

Others found the regular service was sufficient to tempt them to live in the area while still working in London – a thing impracticable before the railway arrived. Among those moving in around this time were four gentlemen cited by E.W. Swanton in his *Bygone Haslemere* as being particularly closely connected with the progress of Haslemere.

John Wornham Penfold (1828–1909), who had been born in the Thursley district of Haslemere and was now surveyor to the Goldsmiths' Company in London, found he was able to return to his old home at Courts Hill. His name is associated with the reconstruction of St Bartholomew's Church after Haslemere became an independent parish, separating from Chiddingfold in 1868; for the hospital on Shepherd's Hill; and for his diligent recording of Haslemere's historical records.

Allen Chandler moved to Haslemere in 1858, and devoted much of his time to local public works, as well as being a JP at the Guildford bench, and noted for his liberal and sympathetic views. His first son, also named Allen, married Ethel, the daughter of Jonathan Hutchinson (see below) in 1887 and thus connected the two families.

James Stewart Hodgson (1827–99) arrived in 1864, and by 1889 had become the largest landowner in the area, owning the Lythe Hill Estate and acquiring the manors of Godalming and Haslemere. He associated himself with the welfare of the "village" (as he always referred to Haslemere), and when faced with financial disaster late in life as a result of troubles in the company with which he was a partner, he sold up and retired with 'fine philosophy' to a small manor house.

Jonathan Hutchinson (1828–1913) had first visited Haslemere

Introduction

on a walking tour in 1863 with his 'crony', the eminent brain specialist John Hughlings Jackson. By 1866, he had decided to make his summer home here at *Inval*, and in 1875 moved there permanently despite his onerous schedule of work as surgeon at the London Hospital during the week. After his wife died in 1887 he launched himself into creating what became, and still remains, the Haslemere Educational Museum.

One can perhaps imagine conversations between these men on the station platform or on the train up to Waterloo – or did they also hide behind their newspapers in those days?

Seal of Approval

While there is no doubt that the men just mentioned made a considerable impact in Haslemere, the outside world heard of the area largely as a result of two other personalities moving here.

Alfred Tennyson (1809–92), Poet Laureate but not yet Lord, was seeking sanctuary. His fame and popularity had caused any number of sightseers (Cockneys as he called them) to seek him out at his home *Farringford* on the Isle of Wight, to such an extent that he no longer felt able to walk outside his garden gate.

He decided to find somewhere more secluded to live, and in the summer of 1866 he and his wife visited Haslemere and the surrounding area looking for land on which to build. After viewing and rejecting a 90 acre site near the Devil's Jumps ("Very dear at the money – what is the use of a number of acres if they will not grow anything?"), he was persuaded by Mrs Anne Gilchrist to rent part of Grayshott Farm (now, considerably enlarged, Grayshott Hall) while he continued his search. "He is very anxious that all this should not be known," she wrote to a friend.

Within a few months, in June 1867, (having first looked at *Meadfield* which Hunter bought some years later) Tennyson found and bought a plot called *Greenhill* which suited him, "in a wooded hollow in Blackdown, on the south side near the top." Here he had *Aldworth* built to his own design. Mrs Gilchrist commented, "I do think if ever there was a place made for a poet to live in, this Green Hill is the spot. Thirty-six acres – half coppice above, three large fields and a little old farmhouse below."

He appears to have been host to many guests at *Aldworth*, but gained the reputation among locals of being wary if recognised and approached as he strode across Blackdown in his black cape

Introduction

and sombrero. Nevertheless, his move to the Haslemere area gave the town and its surrounding countryside one renowned seal of approval.

The second was from Professor John Tyndall (1820–93). Having made his name in the world of physics and also in the world of mountaineering, he was looking for somewhere with good air and convenient to London where he, too, could build himself a house. On analysing the air at Hindhead, he found it to be "as pure as alpine," and decided to move there.

For a while, he and his wife occupied a one-room hut in the middle of the common, "surrounded by the purplest of purple heather." They loved the scenery and seclusion it gave them and, as he wrote to a colleague in August 1883, "though I do not suppose we shall be happier than in our hut, we are aiming at having a house erected by next year. I have already sunk a well, and from it we shall draw water soft as the dew and clear as crystal."

Hind Head House, newly constructed in 1884

They moved into the house in time to celebrate Christmas 1884. Called *Hind Head House* (now converted into flats), it was then the only building on the common. Sadly for Tyndall, he had proclaimed too loudly the great benefits of the area, and others were quick to recognise its advantages. Soon he had neighbours building on adjoining sites, and his peace was disturbed.

To protect himself he bought up as much surrounding land as he could, and when that failed he resorted, in about 1890, to erecting huge screens, 40 feet high, made of larch poles covered with heather and even including lightning conductors. He was very proud of these screens, but his enthusiasm was not shared generally by his friends and neighbours. Furthermore the matter got into the newspapers, especially those hostile to him on political grounds, and the whole affair acquired a great notoriety and was a recurring source of annoyance to him.

Introduction

The screens survived Tyndall, one at least being reported as finally collapsing during the first month of 1901. Tyndall died from an accidental overdose of chloral administered by his wife in December 1893.

Tyndalls screens

Open Spaces and Commoners' Rights

In December 1884, at about the same time that the Tyndalls moved into their new house, some of the more established residents of Haslemere were gathering at the *Swan Inn* to voice their concern over a recent enclosure by the lord of the Manor of Frydinghurst. This related to about 30 acres of Hindhead Common at the top of Farnham Lane, mentioned in some references as Frydinghurst Common.

The meeting was chaired by Stewart Hodgson, who proposed the formation of a Haslemere Commons Committee in order to challenge this and other encroachments more effectively than could be done by individuals. The challenge was to be made in the name of the commoners who claimed to have rights there – including, significantly, Jonathan Hutchinson.

The stated objective of the committee was "to preserve the commons and wasteland in the neighbourhood of Haslemere in their open condition," and Hodgson had already lined up an executive committee to run it, with appropriate terms of reference. It was to include Robert Hunter, who had moved to Haslemere the previous year while continuing also to work long hours in London, and who had by this time made a name for himself in saving Epping Forest from enclosure on behalf of the national Commons Preservation Society. It was he who had suggested the formation of this Haslemere Committee to Hodgson. Along with Hunter stood Charles Puller, Rayner Storr, and the rector, Sanders Etheridge. They were elected unopposed and gave themselves the following brief.

Firstly, they were to endeavour "to obtain the support of landowners and residents in the district, and other persons interested in the preservation of common lands, so that a representative and influential body opposed to enclosure may be constituted." They also proposed "to obtain exact information as

Introduction

to the legal position of the several commons in the neighbourhood, and with the assistance of the published Ordnance Survey to prepare a good map, which will be accessible to residents interested in the question."

In the longer term, they intended "with the assent of the lords of manors, to place some of the more important commons under statutory regulation, and thus more effectually to prevent nuisances and preserve order thereon."

This particular lord of the manor of Frydinghurst eventually submitted to a judgement, dated St George's Day, 23rd April 1888, whereby "the freehold tenants of the manor are declared to be entitled to rights of common, of pasture, of turbary and of estovers," and the lord was prevented from "enclosing or digging gravel to the injury of the tenants' rights." By this means an important portion of Hindhead came under the care of neighbouring residents.

The National Scene

The fight to preserve commons and open spaces from enclosure, and worse, was being pressed strongly across the whole country. In 1865, George Shaw Lefevre (who became Lord Eversley) had founded the national Commons Preservation Society, which began direct action against lords of the manor who attempted to enclose their land.

Two years later, when aged 23 and working as an articled clerk with a firm of solicitors in Holborn, Robert Hunter had entered a competition to write a 15,000 word essay on "Commons and the best means of preserving them for the public." Though not the winner, he was judged to be one of the six best, his text containing such injunctions as: "Any commoner whose rights are molested is clearly entitled to throw down the whole fencing or other obstruction erected." This caught the eye of Shaw Lefevre, and when the post of honorary solicitor to the Society became vacant, he offered it to Hunter.

Here Hunter met Henry Fawcett, then a Liberal MP, and the partnership between these two proved a powerful force within the Society for fourteen years. They are credited with bringing to an abrupt end the previous systematic enclosure of some 25,000 acres of common land each year. Memorably, they saved Epping Forest from enclosure and, following a legal battle which lasted over three years and involved 16 lords of the manor, scores of witnesses and barrow-loads of information, it was finally opened

Introduction

as a Public Park by Queen Victoria in 1882.

But Hunter's acute legal mind was aware that the legislation of the day was not really adequate to deal with all cases where preservation was required. One particular case highlighted the problem. In 1884, the owner of Sayes Court, a 17th century manor house at Deptford, wished to donate it and its grounds to the public, but there was no authority in existence which could accept and maintain it.

After searching for suitable Acts under which this might be achieved, Hunter decided that the only way forward would be to set up a new Company which would have powers to buy and hold land and buildings for the benefit of the nation. He could not do this immediately – indeed it took another ten or so years to achieve – and Sayes Court was left to be demolished. But the germ of the idea for the Company was sown, and grew in time to become The National Trust.

Right to Build

During this same period, Hutchinson had taken the opportunity to buy a number of plots of land in and around Haslemere and build on them. He distrusted stocks and shares, and never invested in anything but land and houses. *Inval*, his original home, was let year on year after 1878 while the family lived successively at one or other of the new houses.

He summed up his attitude to such development in one of his letters to his wife: "I should on principle be prepared to make any sacrifice which would enable a larger number of city residents, for longer periods, to obtain the kind of advantages which we have enjoyed." When a local resident complained about him building on good shooting ground, he commented: "It is a great mistake to think that other people do not enjoy the country, or are not worthy of it; and the desire of the old families about Haslemere to keep it to themselves is simply an unconscious selfishness. Mr W objects to houses on Stoatley because it is such a good partridge ground. Children are more than partridges."

He attended a packed parish meeting when well over eighty years old, to speak in favour of building a road along the ridge of Blackdown. He described the view there as a national asset, and urged that everything should be done to let the greatest number of people enjoy it. He voted but was in a minority of three, with all the town, aristocracy, and tradesmen against him. Writing Hutchinson's biography, his son Herbert comments: "He would

Introduction

have forgiven untidiness, and never said a word against the invasion of the countryside. It was all to the good, and a matter of the greatest possible satisfaction."

Despoiling of Hindhead Common

With the creation of District and Parish Councils in 1894, some of the people most active in promoting the Commons Committee found their time fully occupied with the affairs of these new Councils, and the Commons Committee ceased to meet after 1895. Hunter himself, knighted the previous year for his services to the Post Office, and in the thick of forming the National Trust, was elected chairman of the first Haslemere Parish Council, which met on 2nd January 1895.

However, by 1899 there were grave concerns over what was going on at Hindhead. As the *Surrey Times* put it on 13th May in an article headed 'Despoiling Hindhead Common': "Many residents of Hindhead are not a little annoyed, and certainly very much grieved, at the poor respect which the new lord of the manor is apparently showing for the natural beauty and adornments of Hindhead Common and the Punch Bowl." The lord of the manor was a man named Whitaker Wright, and his destiny is tied intimately to the acquisition by the National Trust of Hindhead Common.

The same article relates that: "Residents have observed the recent visits of gangs of workmen and an 'infernal machine' constructed for this special purpose, with which a holly here and a holly there are lifted bodily from their place with a couple of tons of earth, and carted straight away." This soil was being taken to landscape Lea Park (now Witley Park) where Wright lived. The paper noted that: "It is believed Mr Whitaker Wright has no personal knowledge of what has been and is being done, and it is hoped that when he is informed, no further spoilation will take place."

A Case of Fraud

Whether or not the work stopped is not recorded, but five years later dramatic events of a completely different nature occurred.

Whitaker Wright seems to have been a colourful character. Born in Cheshire, and purposely retaining his north country accent throughout his life, he emigrated to America in 1866 and

Introduction

became an American citizen ten years later. In Philadelphia he married an American girl and had three children. He also made a fortune there – and lost it, returning to England in 1889 because of "some trouble with his companies." But eight years later he had become a millionaire again and acquired, among other things, the Manor of Witley which included Hindhead Common and the Devil's Punch Bowl.

It is said that he kept more than 500 workmen busy with the "improvements" he made to Lea Park. These included a set of three artificial lakes with an underground room under one of them. However, he began to have more "trouble" with his companies over here, and was denounced at an AGM in December 1900 for misuse of invested funds. Slowly but surely his creditors moved against him, and in March 1902 it was decided that he had a case to answer. By this time, sensing trouble, he had gone to live in Paris, and on hearing the news, he took a boat direct from Le Havre to New York, travelling under an assumed name. But the warrant for his arrest preceded him, and he was arrested on landing. He managed to delay extradition for several months, but in September 1902 he was brought back to England to face trial.

Whitaker Wright addressing his shareholders

The trial was held in January 1904, the verdict went against him, and he was given a seven year prison sentence. Prepared for this, Whitaker Wright excused himself, went to the lavatory, and while there slipped a cyanide capsule in his mouth. On coming out, as the *Surrey Advertiser* reports: "He asked for a cigar, and one was given him from his own case. A match was struck, and he was about to light the cigar when he commenced to breathe heavily, and sank into a chair. A doctor was sent for, but a short examination convinced him that death was imminent. Within a quarter of an hour of his being taken ill, he ceased to breathe." Another source states that he also had a loaded revolver on him – obviously he was taking no chances!

Introduction

A Unique Opportunity

As a result of Wright's death, his property was put up for auction by order of the Chancery Division – in fifty lots, since it had not been sold as a whole. Lot 47 was "the manorial rights over Hindhead commons, including Devil's Punch Bowl, Gibbet Hill, etc.: 750 acres, timber included."

As *The Times* reported: "It was to be anticipated that such an opportunity would not be allowed to pass by those who are interested in the preservation of open spaces ... the Commons Preservation Society appealed to the neighbourhood and their appeal met with a warm and ready response."

A local committee was set up, chaired inevitably by Hunter, and its members started to gather names of local people who would guarantee to help fund the purchase of Lot 47.

By the time the auction was held, in Godalming on Thursday 26th October 1905, they had received promises totalling just over £2,200. But would this be sufficient?

"Their Hearts for the Moment Failed"

The sale was attended by Francis Muir and Mr Miller for the committee, and Laurence Chubb who was secretary of the Commons Preservation Society. The purchase was to be made in the name of Mr A M S Methuen. Let Sir Robert Hunter tell you himself how the bidding went:–

"The biddings started at £2,000 and went up very quickly to £3,000, and I am bound to say that the hearts of our representatives for the moment failed. But happily Mr Chubb was able to introduce Mrs Thackeray Turner to Mr Muir and Mr Miller. She with great public spirit and generosity at once said she would be willing to guarantee an additional £500 rather than see this splendid opportunity lost. Upon the basis of that offer the committee proceeded with their bids, and they succeeded in securing the lot at £3,625 – a little over £4 10s per acre."

In fact the reserve had been set at that sum. Speaking just after the event, Hunter noted that their guarantees amounted to £2,922, so that roughly speaking there was a balance of about £700 still to find. It seems they had no difficulty in obtaining this, and the acquisition took place on 30th December 1905.

Introduction

HINDHEAD SAFE
PUBLIC SPIRITED ACTION OF HASLEMERE RESIDENTS

On Friday night last week Sir Robert Hunter announced at a meeting at Haslemere that at the sale of the late Mr Whitaker Wright's property the previous day the Manor of Witley, comprising the Hindhead Commons, Gibbet Hill and the Devil's Punch-bowl had been purchased by a few public spirited persons in that district, and would be preserved in perpetuity for ever.

In 'The Times' of Monday appeared an interesting article on the subject, evidently contributed by someone well acquainted with the district and possibly with all the circumstances connected with the purchase. We can not do better than reproduce the major portion of this article. The writer says:–

Some years ago Mr Whitaker Wright added to his Surrey possessions by the purchase of the manor of Witley. This manor is rich in common land and the lord of the manor is (or to be accurate was till Thursday last) the owner of the soil, not only of the beautiful stretches of gorse, heather and fir which lie to the south of Godalming between the Portsmouth and Chichester road, but also of Hindhead. Hindhead is perhaps the best known of all the Surrey hills. Rising to close on 900ft it commands a wide prospect on all sides. To the east lies the weald of Surrey and Sussex, bordered on the north by the greensand ridge of which Leith Hill is the culminating point and by the North Downs. To the north-west and west the Aldershot country and the rolling chalk hills of Hampshire diversified by such features as Crooksbury, Farnham Castle, the Frensham Ponds and Selborne Hanger; while to the south are the South Downs and the nearer heights of Marley and Blackdown. The hill falls steeply on the Witley side and the thick growth of heather dotted with fine hollies breaks away into woods and coppice. Almost over the summit – now marked by Sir William Erle's quaint cross but, from the ghastly burden it once bore, still called Gibbet Hill – swoops in a long curve the Portsmouth Road, while deep below lies the impressive combe known as The Devil's Punch-bowl. Mr Pepys travelling to Portsmouth on admiralty business found little to admire and much to fear in the road round the Punch-bowl, and Cobbett pronounced Hindhead a God forsaken place; even Turner's sketch gives an awesome aspect to the cloud-capped hill, but professor Tyndall changed all this. Led by his love of alpine air, Tyndall made himself a home on the highest available spot and his example has been followed to such good purpose that Hindhead now boasts its scores of mansions, villas and weekend cottages, its two hotels, many boarding houses, church and public hall. All this building has been made possible by parliamentary enclosure on a large scale, which took place in the middle of the last century. The far-stretching parish of Frensham was wholly enclosed; but the parish of Witley, which comprises the Gibbet Hill and the Punch-bowl, was happily left unchanged. These famous features of Surrey were bought by Mr Whitaker Wright with the other wastes of Witley manor and came to the hammer last Thursday.

THE SURREY ADVERTISER AND COUNTY TIMES
SATURDAY, NOVEMBER 4, 1905

Introduction

In Trust

A local committee was formed to take over the management of the commons from the guarantors, and at their first meeting appointed Hunter as chairman.

It had always been the intention of the purchasers to convey the land to The National Trust, which had been conceived by Hunter for just such a purpose, and this was achieved on 22nd March 1906.

Thus, as the *Surrey Advertiser* announced following the auction: "Hindhead is safe" and would be "preserved in perpetuity for ever."

This confident declaration was given further support the following year, when Parliament passed the National Trust Act of 1907 under which the Trust was given the power to declare land it owned as "inalienable." This protects the property from compulsory purchase by a local authority or by a ministry – it can only be taken by a special Act of Parliament.

Hindhead, in 1906, was the first Trust property in the country to be managed by a local committee. Over the years, further land was acquired nearby, including some in neighbouring Sussex, and in 1908 the large expanse of Ludshott Common in Hampshire was added. This prompted the Trust in time to split the local management around the Haslemere area into three separate committees, one for property in Surrey, one for Sussex and one for Hampshire.

A Summary of National Trust land around Hindhead today

Hampshire: *Ludshott – to the south and west of Hindhead, comprising Bramshott Chase, Ludshott Common, Waggoner's Wells, Gentles Copse and Passfield Common – about 1,000 acres.*

Surrey: *Hindhead – about 1,000 acres of connected common, heath and woodland to the north of Haslemere, including Hindhead, Inval and Weydown Commons, the Devil's Punch Bowl, and the viewpoint of Gibbet Hill, plus a number of detached areas including Golden Valley, Whitmore Vale, Nutcombe Down, Tyndall's Wood and Polecat.*

Introduction

In Memoriam

Sir Robert retired from the Post Office at the end of July 1913. As well as fighting for nearly 45 years to preserve open spaces and places of beauty, he had also masterminded the acquisition of the private telephone companies for the state on behalf of the Post Office. In this he was responsible for passing about fifty Acts through parliament – no mean feat.

Unfortunately his retirement did not last long, and he died of septicaemia less than 4 months later at his home in Haslemere. His funeral in the parish church and a simultaneous memorial service in London were attended by many lords and knights of the realm. In 1919, the beautiful ponds and wooded valley at Waggoner's Wells, adjacent to the Trust land at Ludshott Common, were purchased with money collected by public subscription, and dedicated as a memorial to Sir Robert Hunter who had died in Haslemere six years previously.

The Tunnel

Crossing Hindhead on the journey from London to Portsmouth has never been easy, and there have been several plans suggested to make that part of the journey easier.

In 1826 a new road was cut below the old turnpike track, and this became the A3 trunk road which was an improvement, but an increase in traffic flow in the latter part of the 20th century along with the need for traffic lights at Hindhead crossroads eventually led to congestion and notorious traffic jams.

Various suggestions were put forward to improve things: a viaduct over the valley below the Punch Bowl, a cutting through Hindhead Common (similar to the solution for the Winchester bypass), or a tunnel.

The debate went on for several years, but the National Trust were in favour of the tunnel as being the least disruptive to their property and, although it was the most expensive option, they eventually got their way.

Boring for the tunnel began in 2008 and it was opened to traffic in July 2011.

Introduction

In celebration of the Tunnel

Two projects were commissioned to celebrate to completion of the tunnel, and both included ideas put forward by children from local schools.

The first was to instal a group of oak benches carved to represent the various interests associated with the construction of the tunnel or benefitting from and the easing of congestion.

Five themes were chosen: Landscape, Literature, Museum, Tunnel and Wildlife and each of these was given to a different school to come up with ideas. In the case of Literature, the children at Camelsdale School chose lines from the works of Arthur Conan Doyle, Flora Thompson and Tennyson to surround a quill pen (see below).

These themes were cut into the wood by chain saw, and the resulting ten benches (two for each theme) set up in a circle on flat ground between the car park and the Punch Bowl.

The second project was to carve a 3-ton piece of Portland stone to represent features of Hindhead Common, the Devil's Punch bowl and the tunnel.

The stone being carved in winter; and the final result 'Portal'

Sculptor Jon Edgar chipped away at ideas marked on the stone in multi-coloured felt-tip pens by local schoolchildren. The result named 'Portal' now stands in the path of the old A3.

Biographies

of some of the people mentioned in this book

Biographies

Donaldson, William (c.1811–55)

A Scot, one of the original 'peelers' in London, who after many years police service joined the newly formed Surrey Police Force in 1851. An Inspector at Haslemere in 1855, he was the first officer of the Surrey force to be killed on duty when felled by a railway navvy in Haslemere High Street.

Conan Doyle, Arthur (1859–1930)

Came to live in Hindhead in 1897 for his wife's health, and had *Undershaw* built. Here he 'revived' Sherlock Holmes, and also became involved in local sporting activities. Described as 'a man with a hand that grips you heartily and, in its sincerity of welcome, hurts.' He served as a physician in the 2nd Boer War, and his pamphlet justifying Britain's action earned him a knighthood in 1902.

Conan Doyle

He was one of the first motorists in the area, and in the same year bought a 10HP Wolseley and drove it himself from Birmingham to Hindhead. His wife died in 1906 and is buried in St Luke's, Grayshott, churchyard. A year later, he re-married and moved from the area.

Fawcett, Henry (1833–84)

Blinded by his father in a shooting accident in 1858, he became professor of Political Economy at Cambridge in 1863 and was elected Liberal member for Brighton in 1865. He insisted on full discussion of enclosure Bills in Parliament, and became a leading member of the Commons Preservation Society. He married Millicent Garrett in 1867. As Postmaster General from 1880–84, he introduced postal orders and the parcel post, and took on Hunter as his legal adviser in 1882.

Gilchrist (née Burrows), Anne (1828–85)

Married Alexander Gilchrist in 1851. When he died in 1861, she finished his *Life of Blake,* publishing it in 1862. During this period, she came to live in Shottermill, near Haslemere (in a house *Brookbank* later rented by George Eliot while completing 'Middlemarch' in 1871). Visited by the Tennysons in 1866, she found *Grayshott Farm* for them to rent while they bought land and built *Aldworth*.

Biographies

Hodgson, James Stewart (1827–99)

James Hodgson

Came to Haslemere in 1864 and made it his home by buying the Lythe Hill Estate in 1867, and *Denbigh House* in 1868. The latter he pulled down and built *Lythe Hill* in Tudor style. He acquired the manors of Godalming and Haslemere, becoming the largest landowner in the immediate vicinity. He associated himself with the welfare of the village (as he always liked to think of Haslemere), and lifted it from the lethargy into which it had sunk since the first Reform Bill disenfranchised it. When the company of Baring, in which he was a partner, failed late in his life, he faced the disaster boldly, sold nearly all his estate, and retired to *The Manor House*, sustained by his devoted wife Gertrude.

Hunter, Robert (1844–1913)

Sir Robert Hunter

Born in Camberwell, first child of Robert Lachlan Hunter and his wife Anne. Attended Grammar school, then went to University College, London where he gained B.A. Honours with firsts in Logic and Moral Philosophy. Here he also developed a love of walking and climbing. Encouraged by his father, he enrolled as an articled clerk with a firm of solicitors in Holborn, but he found the work totally uninteresting. To relieve the boredom he read for a Master's degree in his own time. In 1866, Sir Henry Peek offered prizes of £400 for essays on *Commons and the best means of preserving them for the public*. Hunter wrote one of the six best entries, and when a vacancy came up in 1868, the Commons Preservation Society made him their Honorary Solicitor. Here he achieved many successes in saving common land from enclosure, most notably Epping Forest, which Queen Victoria declared open as a public park in 1882. In that same year, he was recommended for the position of Legal Adviser to the Post Office, where he stayed for the rest of his working life, though he still regularly assisted the Society in its work.

In 1883, he and his family moved to Three Gates Lane,

Biographies

Haslemere, where he joined the growing band of rail commuters employed in London. The following year, Octavia Hill enlisted his help in trying to save Sayes Court in Deptford. The owner wanted to give the property to the nation, but no organisation existed to accept the gift. Hunter felt a new 'Company' should be established for such purposes, and so began his idea of a 'National Trust.' The idea lay dormant for nearly 10 years until 1893, when Hardwicke Rawnsley sought help to buy some land in the Lake District which was under threat from speculators. This time the seed grew, and in January 1895 the National Trust was founded, with Hunter as its first chairman. Knighted the previous year for his services to the Post Office, he also became chairman of the first Haslemere Parish Council, formed in the same month as the Trust. This diligent, quiet man retired from the Post Office at the end of July 1913, but by early November had died of septicaemia. Waggoners Wells, near Grayshott, was acquired by the Trust in 1919 and dedicated to his memory.

Hutchinson (née West), Jane (1835–87)

Married to Jonathan in 1856, they had 10 children: Elizabeth, Jonathan, Ethel, Proctor, Llewellyn, Roger, Herbert, Ursula, Agnes, and Bernard. In 1884, Bernard died tragically of tetanus at the age of 9 after grazing his knee while playing in their London garden. Jane never really got over this, and died herself three years later.

Hutchinson, Jonathan (1828–1913)

Born in Selby, Yorkshire, of a Quaker family, he married another Quaker, Jane Pynsent West, in 1856. He first visited Frensham and Hindhead on a walking holiday in 1863, the same year that he was elected a full surgeon to the London Hospital. This post required him to live near the hospital during the week, but the railway allowed him and his family first to rent, and finally buy, property in the Haslemere area.

Sir Jonathan Hutchinson

After his wife's early death, Jonathan, always a keen educationalist, involved himself in a project to create an Educational Museum in Haslemere – it still exists to this day in much the same form as he envisaged it then. He was knighted in 1908, and died peacefully in the library at *Inval* in 1913.

Biographies

Penfold, John Wornham (1828–1909)

Born in Haslemere, he studied architecture and surveying in London and was appointed surveyor to the Goldsmiths' Company. The opening of the railway in 1859 allowed him access to his old home at Courts Hill. In 1866 the post office introduced a road-side pillar box of his design, one of which still functions today in Haslemere High Street. He planned the reconstruction of Haslemere Parish Church in 1870–71, and was also a diligent collector and photographer of Haslemere history.

John W. Penfold

Shaw, George Bernard (1856–1950)

George Bernard Shaw

Shaw's first contact with the district was in 1898 when he leased 'Pitfold' at Woolmer Hill for his honeymoon. He later moved to 'Blencathra' (now St Edmund's School) where he stayed until he left the district in 1900. While there he wrote the third act of *Caesar and Cleopatra* while recovering from a badly sprained ankle. In March 1899 he and Conan Doyle were principal speakers at a Peace Meeting held in Hindhead Congregational Hall where he is reported as delivering at 'vigorous oration'. Flora Thompson says of him in *Heatherley* that: "no-one quite knew what he wrote, but it was known that he was thought a lot of in London. Very clever, they said, very clever indeed" and that she had "several times heard him lecture on Socialism."

Shaw Lefevre, George John (1832–1928)

Born in London, and MP for Reading 1863–85, he served in Liberal ministries in 1881–84 and 1892–95. Was instrumental in forming the Commons Preservation Society in 1865, and was its chairman for many years. Recommended Hunter for the job of legal adviser to the post office, and succeeded Henry Fawcett as Postmaster General (1884–85), introducing the sixpenny telegram. Created Baron Eversley in 1906.

Biographies

Tennyson, Alfred (1809–92)

Alfred Tennyson

Born in 1809, he established his fame as a poet in 1842 and succeeded Wordsworth as Poet Laureate in 1850, the same year that he married Emily Sarah Sellwood. Made their home on the Isle of Wight, but by 1866 he was becoming frustrated with the tourists who came there to seek him out, and started to look for some secluded property on the mainland. He spent the summer of 1866 in this area, and the following year rented *Grayshott Farm* (now *Grayshott Hall*), staying there while he found and purchased suitable land on Blackdown. Here he had *Aldworth* built to his own design, laying the foundation stone on 23rd April 1868. In 1884 he reluctantly accepted a peerage. He died peacefully at *Aldworth* in 1892.

Thompson (née Timms), Flora (1876–1947)

Flora Thompson

Moved to various locations while working for the post office after leaving her native Oxfordshire, and arrived in Grayshott as assistant postmistress and telegraph operator in 1898. She stayed until the Hindhead post office was opened in 1900, whereupon business dropped by 80% and she was moved on again. Her time in Grayshott before leaving the area is recorded in her book *Heatherley*, written near the end of her life and somewhat in the style of her more famous trilogy *Lark Rise to Candleford*.

Tyndall (née Hamilton), Louisa (1845–1940)

Eldest daughter of Lord Claud Hamilton and Lady Elizabeth Proby, she married John Tyndall in 1876 and devoted herself to assisting him with his work. It was a joke between them that they were both people of untidy habits. They kept promising each other to start writing 'their' biography, but mortified by her involvement in John's death, she was unable to complete it herself.

Biographies

Tyndall, John (1820–93)

Born in Co. Carlow, Ireland, he found employment in the Ordnance Survey in 1839. Moved with them to England in 1842, then quitted to become a Railway engineer. In 1847 he started an academic career, and rose to become one of the foremost physicists of his time, being made a fellow of the Royal Society in 1852. His interest in the Alps began in 1856 – he was one of the first to climb the Matterhorn, and the first up the Weisshorn in 1861. He married Louisa in 1876. They moved to Hindhead in 1883 for reasons of his health, living in a single-room hut "surrounded by the purplest of purple heather" while *Hind Head House* was being built. Later he erected 40ft high screens to shield himself from neighbours. He was prescribed magnesia and chloral for his gout. Louisa administered these to him, but in December 1893 accidentally gave him 10 times the proper dose from the wrong bottle, which proved to be fatal. He lies buried in Haslemere churchyard.

John Tyndall

Wright, Whitaker (1845–1904)

One of a large Cheshire family, he crossed the Atlantic in 1866 as a professional assayer and began mining. Had a near scrape with Indians in Idaho – the story goes that some of his workers were killed, but he had endeared himself to a squaw by giving her tobacco, so was spared. Became a naturalised American, married and had 3 children. Had 'some trouble with his companies' and returned to England in 1889, no longer a millionaire, but solvent. In 1897, the FT included him among their 'Men of Millions' again. By 1899 he had bought Lea Park *(now Witley Park)* and Hindhead Common. He began to have more company trouble, and by 1902 was asked to answer in court. He 'bolted for New York' but was arrested on landing and sent back to the UK to face charges of serious fraud. The case went against him, and on

Biographies

26th January 1904 he committed suicide in court, swallowing a cyanide capsule. Despite being a suicide, he is buried beneath an imposing marble slab in the graveyard of All Saints Church, Witley. According to his granddaughter, the family then destroyed all photographs of him and he was never mentioned afterwards.

Calendar of Events

*related to the creation of
The National Trust
and its acquisition of
Hindhead Common*

Calendar

1786 The unknown sailor is murdered on Hindhead
1851 Sir William Erle has the Cross erected on Hindhead
1855 Inspector William Donaldson killed in Haslemere by railway navvies [July 28]
1856 Extensive enclosures of the common lands neighbouring Haslemere
1859 Portsmouth Railway through Haslemere opened to passengers [Jan 1]
1860 John Tyndall climbs the Matterhorn
1862 Anne Gilchrist living in *Brookbank*, Shottermill
1864 James Stewart Hodgson comes to Haslemere
First edition of Surrey Advertiser printed [Apr 3]
1865 Commons Preservation Society (CPS) founded by George Shaw Lefevre
Robert Hunter takes his degree at University College, London
1866 Hunter's was one of the best six essays on "Commons and the best means of preserving them for the public."
Hutchinson makes his summer home in the Haslemere area at *Inval*
The Tennysons visit Anne Gilchrist, looking for local property [Sept 16]
1867 Hodgson buys the Lythe Hill Estate
The Tennysons rent Grayshott Farm *(now Grayshott Hall)* [late Mar]
Article on 'A Visit to Haslemere Fair' – describes it as 'cheerless', and the town still without gas lighting [*Surrey Advertiser – May 18]*
Hunter articled to firm of London solicitors
1868 Tennyson lays foundation stone at *Aldworth* [April 23]
Hunter appointed Hon. Solicitor to the Commons Preservation Society
Haslemere becomes independent parish by separation from Chiddingfold
1869 Anne Gilchrist leaves *Brookbank* (George Eliot arrives in 1871 to complete *Middlemarch*)
First gas lighting in Haslemere

Calendar

1870 Penfold's plans for St Bartholomew's Church begin [July]
1871 St Bartholomew's Church rebuilding completed [July]
1872 Hunter's first wife dies in childbirth
1874 Hunter's Epping Forest case concluded
1875 Hutchinsons move permanently to Haslemere
1876 Tyndall marries Louisa, eldest daughter of Lord Claud Hamilton [Feb 19]
1877 Hunter marries secondly Ellen Cann
1882 Queen Victoria declares Epping Forest open as a public park [May 6]
Hunter recommended for position of legal adviser to the Post Office
1883 The Tyndalls move into their hut at Hindhead
The Hunters come to live at *Meadfield,* Three Gates Lane, Haslemere
1884 Tennyson accepts peerage reluctantly [Jan]
Hutchinson's youngest son Bernard, aged 9, dies of tetanus in London – buried in Haslemere [Apr]
Battle lost to save Sayes Court at Deptford
Address by Hunter on "three distinct perils"
– he proposes here the creation of what became the National Trust [Sept]
Shaw Lefevre becomes Postmaster General (succeeding Fawcett) [Nov 7]
Haslemere Commons Committee of CPS formed [Dec 16]
The Tyndalls spend first night in their new house at Hindhead [Dec 22]
1885 Letter from Octavia Hill to Hunter states her preference for the word "Trust" – Hunter pencils in the words "?National Trust" [Feb 10]
Hutchinson buys land at Hindhead and builds *Trimmer's Wood* there
1886 Tyndall tells Huxley about 'colony of heathens' at Hindhead [May]
1887 Queen's Golden Jubilee – bonfire on Hindhead 'burns all night' [June 21]
Hutchinson's wife dies [Aug 6]

Calendar

1888 Hutchinson begins his Educational Museum at *Inval*
1889 Whitaker Wright returns to England from America
 Hodgson is largest landowner in Haslemere area
 Tennyson writes *Crossing the Bar*
1890 Tyndall speech in Haslemere against Gladstone and Irish Home Rule [Apr 17]
1891 Letters in national press about Tyndall's screens [Sept]
1892 Alfred Lord Tennyson dies at Aldworth [1.35 am, Thurs 6th Oct]
1893 Tyndall dies of accidental Chloral poisoning by his wife [Dec 4]
1894 Hunter knighted for work connected with the Post Office [Jan]
 Hodgson's estates auctioned due to his financial problems – Hutchinson buys Half Moon Estate and starts developing it [July 14]
 Duke of Westminster chairs meeting to form The National Trust [July 16]
 Hunter proposed as Chairman of first Haslemere Parish Council [Dec 8]
1895 First meeting of Haslemere Parish Council – Hunter in chair [Jan]
 The National Trust registered under the Companies Act [Jan 12]
 First lecture given in the new Haslemere Museum [Sunday 18th Aug]
1896 Conan Doyle takes *Grayswood Beeches* at Hindhead for the summer [July]
1897 Diamond Jubilee year – the population of Haslemere reaches 2,000
 Whitaker Wright one of the six "Men of Millions" (*FT*)
1898 Conan Doyle moves to *Undershaw* [October]
 George Bernard Shaw first comes to the district on honeymoon
 Flora Thompson (Timms) arrives in Grayshott as assistant postmistress [Sept]

Calendar

1899 Report on 'despoilation' of Hindhead *(Surrey Advertiser)* – Whitaker Wright new lord of the manor [May 13]

1901 Queen Victoria dies; Tyndall's screen finally falls [Jan 21]

1902 Whitaker Wright 'bolts' for the USA under an assumed name – arrested on landing [Mar]

Conan Doyle drives his new Wolseley from Birmingham to Hindhead and in same year is knighted for supporting the Government on Boer War

1904 Whitaker Wright commits suicide at court in London [Jan 26]

1905 Local decision to purchase Hindhead Common [Oct 14]

Hindhead Common purchased at auction in Godalming [Oct 26]

1906 Hindhead Common conveyed to the NT [Mar 22]

1907 NT becomes a statutory body legalised by Act of Parliament

1908 Hutchinson knighted for his services to medicine [June]

1913 Hutchinson dies peacefully – buried next to wife and son in Haslemere churchyard – "A man of hope and forward-looking mind" [June 23]

Hunter retires from the Post Office [July 31]

Hunter dies of septicaemia – buried at Haslemere parish church [Nov 6]

1919 Waggoners Wells acquired by NT and dedicated to Hunter [Dec]

Dramatic Walks

The Devil's Punch Bowl in 1938

Over Hindhead Common

Acknowledgements

My thanks to Diana Hawkes, curator of Haslemere Educational Museum in 1994, for the original idea of the Hindhead walk, to Thelma Ede for helping with the research and to The National Trust for their assistance in staging the event.

The cast for the opening performance in April 1995 was:—

Sir Robert Hunter	John Owen Smith
Professor John Tyndall	Noël Diacono
Mrs Louisa Tyndall	Diana Hawkes
Highwaymen	Amanda Lane & Ann McLaughlin
Sir Jonathan Hutchinson	Tony Grant
Mrs Jane Hutchinson	Adrienne Robb
Alfred, Lord Tennyson	Anthony Elliott
Broomsquire	Andrew Storey (NT Warden)
Broomsquire's wife	Eve Phillips
Sailor	Chris Webb
Murderers	Tony Grant & Derek Watts
Witnesses	Andrew Storey & Eve Phillips
Sir Arthur Conan Doyle	Noël Diacono

The cast in August 2010 was:—

Sir Robert Hunter	John Owen Smith
Professor John Tyndall	Rod Sharp
Mrs Louisa Tyndall	Wendy Downs
Highwayman	Luke Oates
Sir Jonathan Hutchinson	David Burnham
Mrs Jane Hutchinson	Tina Wareham
Alfred, Lord Tennyson	Paul Wareham
Broomsquire	Bill Westbroek (NT Warden)
Broomsquire's Wife	Kay McGregor
Sailor	Nick Webb
Michael Casey	Peter Glinn
James Marshall	Johnny Preskett
Edward Lonigon	Martin Wellen
Witnesses	Penny McKay, Dil Williamson-Smith
Sir Arthur Conan Doyle	Louis Clist

Over Hindhead Common

Introduction

On the last day of April 1995, in the centenary year of the National Trust, an estimated 300 people gathered by the Devil's Punch Bowl Hotel. They were to take part in the inauguration of the Sir Robert Hunter Trail on Hindhead Common.

'Sir Robert Hunter' arrived in person, and led the cavalcade on the walk. He stopped at a number of points to tell the assembled company a little of the history of the area and the personalities who frequented it. Scenes were acted out in front of the crowd by a troupe of actors, including some local National Trust Wardens and the curator of Haslemere Museum. Most dramatically, two highwaymen on horses suddenly sprang from a side track and held up some unfortunate travellers.

The walkers met in turn Professor & Mrs John Tyndall, Sir Jonathan Hutchinson and his wife, Lord Tennyson, Sir Arthur Conan Doyle, a pair of broomsquires complete with besoms, and of course the unfortunate sailor and his villainous murderers.

Since then the 'dramatic walk' has been performed again several times on a fairly regular basis.

Here we trace the route and include the original script used by the actors. We also give information relating to the personalities and scenes portrayed, to help if you wish to pursue further studies yourself.

Why not take the trail with a group and re-enact some of the scenes?

Over Hindhead Common

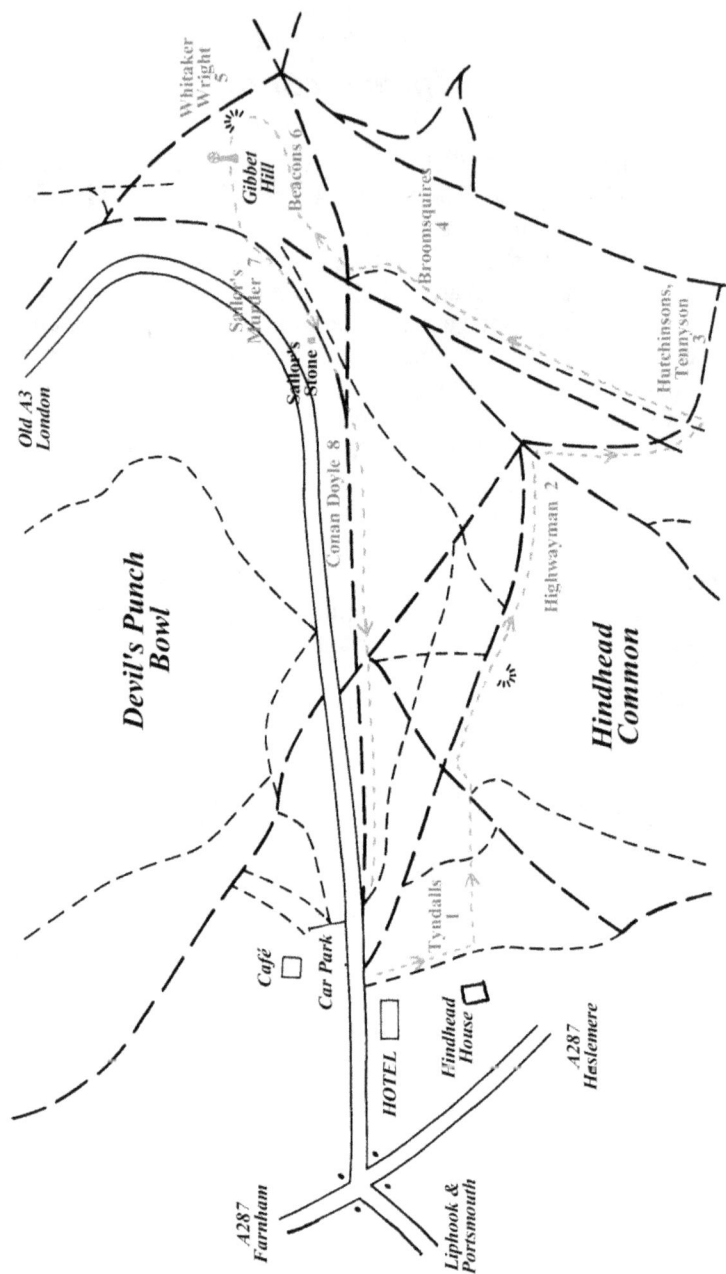

Over Hindhead Common
showing where the scenes take place

Over Hindhead Common

Scene 1 Professor Tyndall appears, and hails Hunter

> **The year is 1891**
>
> Starting by the side of the Devil's Punch Bowl Hotel (see map), follow the path down the side of Hindhead Common to arrive at the rear of Hindhead House. When Tyndall built it in 1884 he 'revelled in its stillness and repose,' but by 1891 he was erecting screens to protect his privacy from others wishing to move here and share the 'purest air this side of the Alps.' We may imagine him coming out of his back gate to greet Hunter as we approach.

Tyndall Ah, there you are Hunter. Glad I've found you.

Hunter Professor Tyndall! How are you, sir?

Tyndall Touch of gout again, but I thought a short walk today would do me no harm. *(Looking at the walkers)* These friends of yours, are they?

Hunter My walking companions today, yes.

Tyndall Not come to buy up more of the land round my house?

Hunter You know I, of all people, would hardly be bringing land speculators round, professor.

Tyndall Dashed nuisance they are! I came here for peace and quiet, and to enjoy breathing the purest air this side of the Alps. Mine was the only house up here when I built it six years ago in '84 – couldn't see another for miles – and then what happened?

Hunter I fear you advertised your views on the benefits of living at Hindhead too well. Others followed your example.

Tyndall How can one concentrate on doing serious work when there's some Londoner busy building – right in front of your study window?

Hunter Well quite, I…

Tyndall Is it any wonder I had to erect screens to protect my privacy?

Hunter The screens were, perhaps, slightly on the large side, professor.

Professor John Tyndall

Born 2nd Aug 1820 in Co. Carlow, Ireland, John Tyndall found employment in the Ordnance Survey in 1839. He moved to England with them in 1842, then quitted to become a Railway engineer for three years. In 1847 he started an academic career, and rose to become one of the foremost physicists of his time, being made a fellow of the Royal Society in 1852.

His interest in the Alps began in 1856 – he was one of the first to climb the Matterhorn 1860, and the first to climb the Weisshorn a year later.

Louisa Tyndall (née Hamilton) was born in 1845, the eldest daughter of Lord Claud Hamilton. She married John in 1876.

They moved to Hindhead in 1883 for reasons of his health, living here in a single-room hut "surrounded by the purplest of purple heather" while Hindhead House was built, and moving into the house just before Christmas 1884. At the time he had no other neighbours, but soon others bought land and built nearby, prompting Tyndall to erect his infamous screens.

In order to alleviate his sufferings from gout, Tyndall's doctor prescribed magnesia and chloral, which Louisa administered to him. However, in December 1893 she accidentally gave him a dose from the wrong bottle, and this proved to be fatal. He lies buried in Haslemere churchyard.

Over Hindhead Common

Tyndall Large? They were only as large as I needed to stop myself being deafened and distracted.

Hunter 40 ft high, I believe.

Tyndall Indeed. Things of beauty and noble structures they are too. Larch poles covered in heather – to blend in with the surroundings.

Hunter Well blend they may, but...

Tyndall They've even got lightning conductors to protect them – I've no concerns about them – they'll not fall down in the wildest storm.

Hunter Your enthusiasm for them has not been shared generally by your friends and neighbours.

Tyndall It's the Tory press – they're against me on political grounds – trying to stir up trouble.

Hunter You gave another speech against Gladstone down in Haslemere only the other week, did you not?

Tyndall I'm against the man *and* his Home Rule Bill for Ireland, as you know.

Mrs Tyndall appears

Mrs Tyndall John, I thought I'd find you out walking. You should be resting you know.

Tyndall *(To Hunter)* Louisa's more than just a wife to me, Mr Hunter – she's my scribe, my clerk, my nurse, my constant companion...

Mrs Tyndall And having precious little effect at the moment. *(Acknowledging Hunter)* Good day to you, Mr Hunter.

Hunter Good day, Mrs Tyndall.

Mrs Tyndall *(To Tyndall)* Dr Winstanley has prescribed draughts of magnesia and syrup of chloral – and it's past time for your next dose.

Tyndall *(To Hunter)* For the conqueror of the Matterhorn and the Weisshorn, it has come to this.

Hunter But the work of the famed physicist, colleague of Faraday and Huxley, carries on undaunted as before, I am sure.

Mrs Tyndall *(To Hunter)* We are about to write our biography.

Tyndall We have been 'about to write our biography' for as long as I can remember.

Mrs Tyndall This evening we will make a start.

Over Hindhead Common

Tyndall Enjoy your walk, Mr Hunter, and *(to the walkers)* to you all. I must return to my retreat.

Hunter Good day to you Professor Tyndall – Mrs Tyndall. *(They return to Hindhead House)*

Follow the winding path opposite the rear entrance of Hindhead House through trees and through a kissing gate to reach open country, then turn left and follow the main track across the common. There are views of the South Downs to your right. It is now the 1920s. At the top of a rise, Hunter meets Flora Thompson on one of her rambles.

Audience listening to 'Sir Robert', August 2010

Flora Thompson

While she was assistant postmistress in Grayshott (1898–1900) and not yet married or famous, Flora Thompson tells us in her book 'Heatherley' that she walked over Hindhead Common with friends "chanting in unison the quatrains of Omar Khayyám, or a chorus from Swinburne, or talking sense or nonsense."

   At the summit, by the Cross, she "dropped to her knees on the turf and, pressing her ear to the cold stone of the shaft, recited in trance-like tones an imaginary conversation between the malefactors who had once suffered there – an effort which was applauded as worthy of Poe."

Over Hindhead Common

> As you come down the hill towards the point where several tracks intersect, imagine a highwayman suddenly springing out at you from behind the shrubbery. **It is the early 1790s**

Scene 2 The highwayman appears

Hunter *(To walkers)* I think we should keep back!

Luke Oates as the Highwayman, August 2010

As the 'hold up' proceeds, Hunter explains…

The Rev James Fielding was appointed curate of Haslemere in 1786, and also became Justice of the Peace in the town, thus holding a very strong, almost unassailable, position in the community there.

He had three daughters and a wife, but apparently home and parish duties weren't enough to keep him occupied, and he was strongly suspected of being involved in highway robbery – either holding up travellers himself or, more likely, employing others to do so.

Mail bags were found hidden in his cellar at *Town House* in Haslemere High Street, and brass plates from mail bags were also found at *Chase Farm*, another of his houses situated conveniently on the county border with Sussex.

However, Fielding was never charged with these crimes and, unlike some of his men who were caught and executed, he died peacefully in his bed.

Over Hindhead Common

> From the intersection, follow the main path bearing round to the right, crossing the track of the old Farnham Lane in about 100 metres. This was once a road to Portsmouth. Continue to the seat overlooking Coombeswell valley.
>
> ### The year is 1866
>
> Here we may meet Jonathan Hutchinson and his wife climbing up one of the steep paths from the house called *Inval*, which they have rented this summer.

Professor Jonathan Hutchinson

Born 23rd July 1828 in Selby, Yorkshire, of a Quaker family, Jonathan Hutchinson married another Quaker, Jane Pynsent West, in 1856. They had 10 children: Elizabeth, Jonathan, Ethel, Proctor, Llewellyn, Roger, Herbert, Ursula, Agnes, and Bernard.

Hutchinson had visited Frensham and Hindhead on a walking holiday in 1863, the same year that he was elected a full surgeon to the London Hospital. This post required him to live near the hospital during the week, but he loved the fresh air here, and the railway allowed him and his family first to rent, and finally buy, property in the Haslemere area for weekends and holidays.

In 1884 their youngest child, Bernard, died tragically of tetanus. Jane never really got over this, and died herself three years later. Jonathan, always a keen educationalist, involved himself in a project to create an Educational Museum in Haslemere – a museum that still exists to this day in much the same form as he envisaged it.

He was knighted in 1908, and died peacefully in 1913.

Over Hindhead Common

Scene 3
The walkers arrive at a viewpoint over Coombeswell – the Hutchinsons appear from below

Hutchinson Well, my dear Jane, does not this countryside please thee? Is it not a solace after the smoke of London?

Mrs Hutchinson Very much better, Jonathan. And the children will enjoy it too.

Hutchinson But perhaps thou shouldst not have climbed up here in thy present condition…

Mrs Hutchinson Nonsense, I am perfectly fit. Having had five children, I believe I know what I *can* do and *cannot* do while expecting a sixth.

Hutchinson So I see. Still, it is a long way up from our house in the valley.

Mrs Hutchinson I have never felt fitter. It is the air here.

Hutchinson We shall have to keep the London property as well, of course – I must live within reach of the Hospital during the week…

Mrs Hutchinson But with the railway to Haslemere, we can come here when we wish. It's only an hour and a half from London.

Hutchinson When I retire we can live here all the time.

Mrs Hutchinson *(Suddenly)* Jonathan, look! *(She points through the trees)* Is that not… The Poet Laureate?

(Tennyson can be seen walking past in the middle distance)

Hutchinson Tennyson? I was told he has been seen rambling around here – looking for some land to buy, to build a house.

Mrs Hutchinson Doesn't he look every bit the poet? Long hair, long cloak and black hat.

Hutchinson He is not coming this way, it seems.

Mrs Hutchinson But perhaps if he buys land here we may have him for a neighbour. How would that be?

Over Hindhead Common

Hutchinson We should not see much of him. I believe he seeks only solitude.

Mrs Hutchinson Whereas thy creed would bring every London waif and ragamuffin out here to populate the heaths and commons.

Hutchinson I feel it is every man's right, whatever his station in life, to enjoy God's healthy countryside as we do. Those that would keep it to themselves are being unconsciously selfish.

Mrs Hutchinson Thou art a devotee of Mr Tennyson's work, though – our family has heard thee declaim it to us often enough.

Hutchinson I have no quarrel with Mr Tennyson – it is the old established families who would rather see partridges here than children. They must learn that children are worth more than partridges.

Alfred Tennyson

Born in 1809, Tennyson established his fame as a poet in 1842 and succeeded Wordsworth as Poet Laureate in 1850, the same year that he married Emily Sarah Sellwood.

He made his home on the Isle of Wight, but by 1866 he was becoming frustrated with the tourists who came there to seek him out, and started to look for some secluded property on the mainland.

He spent the summer of 1866 in this area, and the following year rented Grayshott Farm (now Grayshott Hall), staying there while he found and purchased suitable land on Blackdown. He had Aldworth built there to his own design, laying the foundation stone in April 1868.

In 1884 he reluctantly accepted a peerage, and died at Aldworth in 1892.

Over Hindhead Common

> Follow the well-defined footpath north-eastwards and slightly uphill through the trees.
>
> **It is the 1860s**
>
> In a few hundred metres you come to a site used in the play as the Broomsquire's camp.

Scene 4 A Broomsquire is making besoms; his wife approaches the walkers

Broomsquire's Wife *(To the walkers)* Nice birch and heather besoms. New brooms to sweep your floors clean – only thruppence each.

Broomsquire Afternoon to ye, ladies and gentlemen. You've been lucky enough to meet up with Edward Moorey, broomsquire to the Royalty. I supply the Duchess of Kent – the old Queen Mother herself – with besoms.

Broomsquire's Wife Takes them all the way up to Lunnun himself he does…

Broomsquire Wouldn't trust anyone else to do it, not I – not to supply Royalty.

Broomsquire's Wife Sometimes he sells the horse and cart when he gets there too, and has to walk back.

Broomsquire Worth it though Ann, worth the journey. 'By Appointment,' I am – I has it written on me cart, I do.

Broomsquire's Wife So who'll buy a Royal broom? You won't get one this quality anywhere else. Quality fit for a queen it is. Cheap at twice the price.

Business ensues with the walkers, who may indeed buy brooms

Broomsquire's Wife Bless you sir, madam.

> Continue along the footpath through a gate and cross the meeting of several tracks, striking out towards the brow of the hill and the triangulation point.
>
> **The year is 1905**

Over Hindhead Common

Scene 5 The walkers arrive at the viewpoint on Gibbet Hill

Hunter Looking from the highest point of Hindhead we have a glorious view over many miles – indeed, on a clear day one can see some of the taller buildings in London.

In 1905, all of Hindhead Common and most of the land immediately below us towards Witley was owned by the then lord of the manor, a man named Whitaker Wright.

Now Mr Wright, though born in the north of England, in Cheshire, had emigrated to America in 1866, made a fortune there, married, had two sons and become an American citizen. Then something went wrong with his companies, and he came back to this country with his family in 1889 – no longer a millionaire, though still solvent.

Eight years later, in 1897, the *Financial Times* included him in a list of millionaires again, so he obviously hadn't lost his touch. It was about this time that he bought the Manor of Witley, and then, bit by bit, other land surrounding it, including Hindhead Common where we stand now.

In a local newspaper article of 1899, entitled "The Despoilation of Hindhead", he is accused of sending in gangs of men with an 'infernal machine' to cart away earth, a couple of tons at a time, and take it down to Witley Park where he was making improvements.

However two years later, in 1901, he was in more serious trouble – accused of fraud in his business dealings. He fled with his family, first to France, and then by boat to America, but was arrested on landing at New York. He managed to delay extradition for several months, but eventually, in January 1904, was brought up for trial at the High Court in London.

The verdict went against him and he was given a 7 year custodial sentence. Rather than face that, he secretly swallowed a cyanide capsule which he had hidden about his person, washed it down with a glass of whisky, we're told, and died within 15 minutes. Very dramatic. He was also found to have a loaded Smith & Wesson revolver in his pocket, so he was obviously taking no chances!

His estate then came up for auction, and a group of local men, myself included, decided to put in a bid for Hindhead Common

Over Hindhead Common

to protect it for the future. I'm glad to say we succeeded, just, and it was transferred to the safe keeping of the National Trust in January 1906.

Scene 6 The summit area

Hunter Now behind us, over here *(indicating the open summit)* we have an area which in the past has been used for many things.

Hilltops have been put to use from time immemorial to send signals of various kinds. The earliest form would be by lighting a fire, but although this hill is so prominent, it seems that others in the locality, such as Blackdown, were generally used in preference. They were in a better position to form a chain of signal stations.

Nevertheless, whenever there is a major national celebration we light a bonfire here. There was a big one in 1887, for example, on the occasion of Queen Victoria's Golden Jubilee; one in 1977 for your Elizabeth II's Silver Jubilee; and one in 1988 to celebrate the 400th anniversary of the defeat of the Spanish Armada.

In 1885, a new sort of signalling station was erected here. It was a heliograph, sending messages by the light of the sun. They were read 13 miles away on Hungry Hill near Ripley, or at least they should have been, but on the opening day smoke from heath fires prevented it. No sign of this construction exists now.

Then during your last war, the army set up an experimental radar station here, although for security reasons it was called an anti-aircraft battery. Engineers concreted the roads to bring equipment up here. Now all that has gone too.

> Move over to the Cross, noting the interpretation board on the way which gives details of its history.

Over Hindhead Common

Hunter Here you'll notice Sir William Erle's cross, erected in 1851 – that's seven years after I was born – on the site of the old gibbet. The inscription in Latin reads:

> POST TENEBRAS LUX
> IN OBITU PAX
> IN LUCE SPES
> POST OBITUM SALUS

which translated means: "After the darkness, light; In death, peace; In light, hope; After death, salvation."

Up until 1826, when a new cutting was made further down the hill, the Portsmouth road ran close to this spot – the track is still there. It was narrow, winding, and bordered by open land, with a steep drop down into the Punch Bowl on one side. Many a grim tale could be told of passages over Hind Head in those days.

The most famous of these concerns a sailor who was walking along the road in September 1786. Sailors then often walked between London and Portsmouth, but this one fell in with three other men, having bought them drinks at the old Red Lion in Thursley. Let's look at the spot where it might have happened....

Over Hindhead Common

> Proceed past the Cross and down the rough paths to the track of the old Portsmouth Road.
>
> **It is September, 1786.** Four men appear, walking up the road together from the direction of Thursley. As the men approach, we hear them in conversation.

Scene 7 The Sailor's murder

Sailor So, Michael Casey, you claim to be one of my shipmates of old. I can't say I remember you.

Casey It was some time ago. I remember your face well, but not your name.

Sailor And your friends here, you're all bound for Portsmouth?

Casey Aye, back to sign on again – but we've not been as careful with our money as you have. Ours is all spent.

Sailor Careful? Fortunate more like.

Casey You mean you came upon the money by chance?

Marshall Gambling, perhaps.

Lonegan Or maybe you stole it.

Sailor Ask no questions, I'll tell you no lies. At least I've been generous enough to buy you drinks at the last two taverns.

Casey So you have.

Marshall You've enough there to buy us drinks at all the taverns from here to Portsmouth.

Lonegan And have sovereigns to spare.

Sailor Luck, my friends.

Casey Well, you won't mind sharing your luck with your old shipmates, will you?

Sailor There's only one of you reckons to be my old shipmate.

Casey But we're all in this together *(significantly, to Marshall and Lonegan)* aren't we my brave boys?

Marshall We're with you Michael.

Lonegan Just say the word.

Sailor *(Uneasily)* We agreed to keep each other company on the road, did we not?

Casey So we did. But we'll keep the company, and you can keep the road. *(He draws a knife, and the other two follow suit)*

Sailor Villains!

They surround him

Casey *(To the others)* Down the slope – we'll do him there.

The sailor is dragged off the road – there they stab him until he is still

Casey *(Comes back to the road and looks around)* Right, bring his things and we'll be off before someone comes. Is the body hidden Jimmy?

Marshall *(Appears carrying clothes)* Ted's just doing that now.

Lonegan appears, also carrying some of the sailor's belongings

Casey Did you hide him well, Ted?

Lonegan I did that, Michael – he'll not be found quickly.

Casey Right, then let's make ourselves scarce.

They walk quickly off along the road towards Portsmouth. As they go, two villagers appear out of hiding.

Villager 1 Mercy, did you see that!

Villager 2 Have they gone?

Villager 1 Aye, they've gone. Quick – over there and see what's happened.

They go over to where the sailor has been left

Over Hindhead Common

Villager 2 You keep guard – I'll go down. *(He disappears)*

Villager 1 See anything? *(Pause)* I say, see anything?

Villager 2 *(Calling back, urgently)* I'm coming back!

Villager 1 What's down there?

Villager 2 *(Arriving, looking sick)* His head – nearly hacked off – it's too horrible to describe!

Villager 1 He's dead then?

Villager 2 What are you, stupid or something?

Villager 1 *(Looking the way the murderers have gone)* Shouldn't we follow them?

Villager 2 What, and end up like that? No, I'm back off down to Thursley. Raise the alarm there. *(He sets off)*

Villager 1 Wait – I'll come with you!

They both hurry off in the direction of Thursley

Hunter Michael Casey (42), James Marshall (24) and Edward Lonegan (26) were pursued down the Portsmouth road by a group of men from Thursley, and arrested at *The Sun Inn* at Rake. They were tried at Kingston and sentenced to be hanged – here, at the scene of their crime – on 7th April 1787. After they were dead, their bodies were tarred and hung up in chains on a thirty foot gibbet, as a warning to others.

Sir William Erle erected his Cross some 65 years later, after the gibbet had disappeared, to bring light and hope to a dark and gloomy place.

The remains of the sailor were buried in Thursley churchyard, and a memorial stone set up by the side of the old Portsmouth road – we shall pass it shortly on the right.

Over Hindhead Common

Walk up the old Portsmouth Road in the direction of Portsmouth. After about a hundred metres you come to the Sailor's Stone on your right.

The Sailor's Stone

This stone was first erected here, according to the inscription, by order of James Stilwell in 1786, soon after the murder was committed. When the new turnpike route was cut in 1826, the stone was removed by the turnpike trustees for renovation and replaced by the side of their new road.

Mr Stilwell's nephew objected to this, and restored it to its original position, adding an engraving on the back: "Cursed be the Man who injureth or removeth this stone.". The trustees then erected a mock stone beside their road – so for a while there were two Sailor's Stones in existence.

The mock stone was almost immediately vandalised, and by 1889 had disappeared. The original was in that year again renovated by Stilwell's heir, as shown by a further inscription on the back. Some time later it was moved back down to the new road – but in 1932 it was returned to its original (and final?) resting place, here where you see it. .

Over Hindhead Common

> Continue along the old Portsmouth Road in the same direction. **It is the year 1902.**
>
> As we approach the village of Hindhead again, we may imagine Sir Arthur Conan Doyle, newly knighted, walking down the track towards us.

Scene 8 Sir Arthur Conan Doyle approaches

Conan Doyle Sir Robert, how nice to meet you taking the air.

Hunter And you too, Mr Conan Doyle. Pardon, <u>Sir</u> Arthur now, is it not – congratulations on your knighthood.

Conan Doyle Thank you. The government seemed to approve of my comments on the Boer War.

Hunter May I introduce you to my party of friends – Sir Arthur Conan Doyle, celebrated resident of Hindhead.

Conan Doyle Delighted to meet you all. Truth to tell, the area seems to be sinking under the weight of celebrated residents.

Hunter I agree. Artists, writers, scientists, politicians…

Conan Doyle I've heard it referred to both as 'Mindhead' and as the 'Lesser Parnassus'.

Hunter I believe you have just taken delivery of a new automobile, Sir Arthur.

Conan Doyle '*Taken* delivery?' – no, my dear Sir Robert, I delivered it myself – drove my Wolseley all the way here from Birmingham.

Hunter Quite a journey.

Conan Doyle The automobile is coming of age. Such journeys no longer seem incredible. I can foresee a time when a man will think no more of owning an automobile than a horse and carriage. Driving to the other end of the country will seem normal.

Hunter I'm not so sure – can you see every coaching inn storing gasoline as well as hay? For that's what it would need, surely.

Conan Doyle For a man of your foresight, Sir Robert, I am surprised you cannot see what I can imagine – the turnpikes filled with horseless carriages.

Over Hindhead Common

Hunter I hope you will not feel me backward if I continue to use horsepower of the animal variety, Sir Arthur.

Conan Doyle With all the dangers that entails, remember – I seem to recall Lady Hunter was tipped from her dog cart a few months back, was she not?

Hunter True, and suffered quite serious injuries at the time, though she is fully recovered now I'm happy to say.

Conan Doyle I am very glad to hear it. But, I rest my case, sir. There are far more accidents caused by horses than by automobiles. The car is a safer form of transport.

Hunter I suspect that may be simply because there are fewer of them.

Conan Doyle Ah, I see Holmes would not get the better of your logical mind, Sir Robert. Well, if you do not mind, I shall continue now with my constitutional.

Sir Arthur Conan Doyle

Born in 1859, he moved to Hindhead in 1898 for his wife's health, building 'Undershaw' near the Hindhead cross roads.

Here he started to write Sherlock Holmes stories again, due to public demand, having killed off his famous detective in a previous book. However he also became closely involved in village life, being active in local cricket and football clubs.

He served as a physician in the 2nd Boer War, and his pamphlet "The War in South Africa" justifying Britain's action earned him a knighthood in 1902.

In that same year he took delivery in Birmingham of a 10HP Wolseley car, which was "smart in dark green with red wheels and could carry five people or seven at a pinch" and weighed nearly a ton. He drove it all the way from Birmingham to Hindhead himself, and was greeted here by a large crowd as his car "chugged along the road amid barking dogs."

His wife died in 1906 and is buried in the churchyard at St Luke's, Grayshott. A year later he re-married and moved to Crowborough where he died in 1930.

Over Hindhead Common

He starts to pass by

Hunter You won't forget the meeting next week, will you – about the Hindhead Common Fire Brigade?

Conan Doyle *(As he parts)* I shall not – I shall be there – until then… *(He lifts his hat and walks on)*

Hunter *(To the walkers)* When a man of Sir Arthur's vision predicts turnpikes filled with automobiles, you have to wonder if he might not be proved right!

> Return to your start point along the old Portsmouth Road.

View over the Devil's Punch Bowl c.1900

Waggoners Wells in reflective mood

Around Waggoners Wells

Acknowledgements

Based on the original idea of the Hindhead walk, we designed a similar dramatic walk around Waggoners Wells to celebrate the centenary of the acquisition of Ludshott Common by the National Trust in 1908.

My thanks to Friends of Ludshott Common and to The National Trust for their assistance in staging the event, and to members of Headley Theatre Club for their enthusiastic performances.

The cast for the opening performance in July 2008 was:—

Sir Robert Hunter	John Owen Smith
Sir Arthur Conan Doyle	Peter Glinn
George Bernard Shaw	Rod Sharp
Broomsquire	Chris Webb (NT warden)
Broomsquire's wife	Kay McGregor
Flora Thompson	Mel White
Alfred, Lord Tennyson	David Burnham
World War 1 veteran	John McGregor
William Cobbett	Nick Webb
Cobbett's squire	Steve White
Canadian WW2 soldier	Jamie Stickler
Mob	Oliver Burnham, Jo Levy, Paul & Tina Wareham

For images of all Sir Robert's Dramatic Walks,
see www.headley-village.com/drama

Introduction

'Sir Robert Hunter' leads the audience on the walk. He stops at a number of points to tell the assembled company a little of the history of the area and the personalities who frequented it. Scenes are acted out in front of the crowd by a troupe of actors.

The walkers meet in turn Sir Arthur Conan Doyle, George Bernard Shaw, a pair of broomsquires complete with besoms, Flora Thompson by the wishing well, Alfred Lord Tennyson, William Cobbett and a lost Canadian soldier from WW2. They are also assailed by a group of Commoners demanding their Commoners' Rights and witness the assault of an innocent trader on his way home from market.

Since 2008 the 'dramatic walk' has been performed a number of times, including in 2019 to commemorate the centenary of the year in which the Ponds were dedicated to Sir Robert's memory.

Why not take the trail yourself and re-enact the scenes?

Wakeners Wells

Waggoners Wells were called Wakeners Wells until fairly recently, seemingly named after a local family called Wakener – an Isabel de Wakener is mentioned in a Pipe Roll of 1309.

In 1623 the Ludshott Manor rolls state that: *"Henry Hooke [Lord of Bramshott & Chiltley manors] has made 2 new pools near Wakeners Well, whence [ie. by so doing] he has flooded part of the waste of this Manor and part of the waste of his own manor [the Waggoners Wells stream was and is the boundary between Ludshott & Bramshott manors], to the loss of the Lord of this manor and his tenants."* One assumes that this did not make him popular with the Commoners!

Hooke had ironworks in nearby Hammer Vale and it's assumed that he was intending to expand his business here – but he died in 1640 and there is no indication that these new 'hammer ponds' were ever used by him. Instead they have now become attractive fish and wildlife ponds.

Around Waggoners Wells

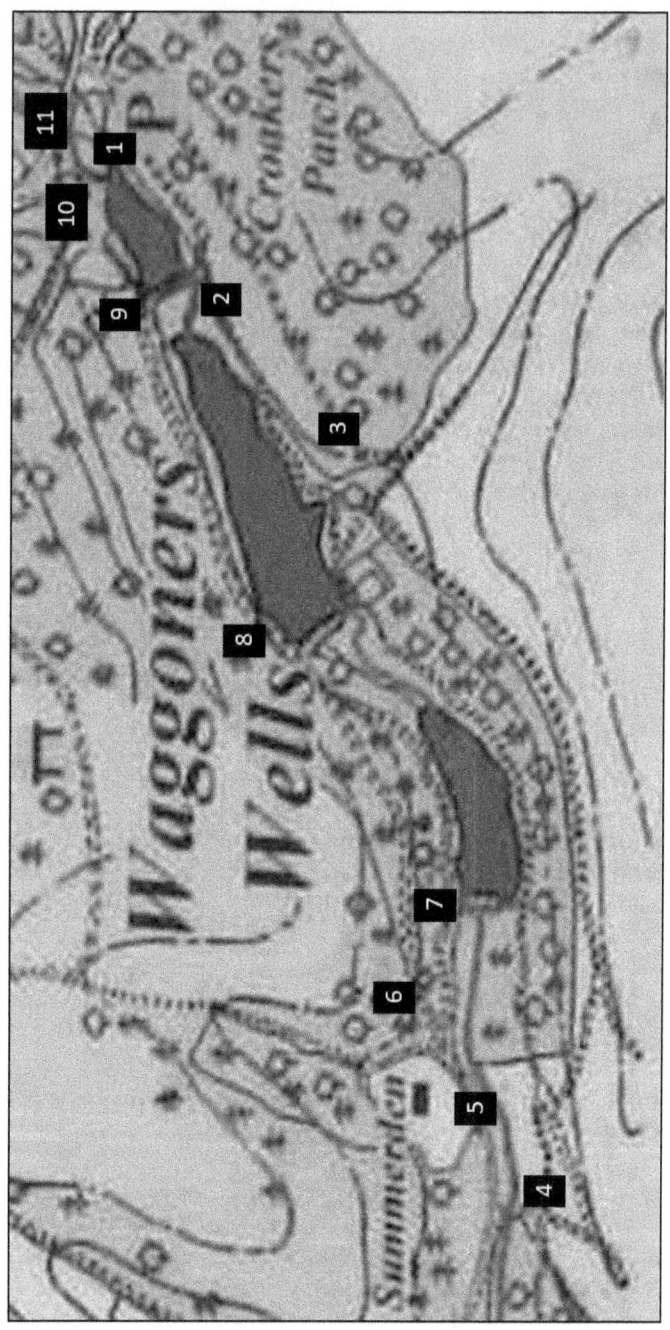

Around Waggoners Wells
showing where the scenes take place

Around Waggoners Wells

> From the car park, go down the steps to the top pond.
> **The year is 1899**

Scene 1 We encounter George Bernard Shaw and Arthur Conan Doyle in earnest discussion

Shaw To be sure, I've never seen anything so abysmal in my life. Never.

Doyle It received a great deal of praise in the local press.

Shaw It did, and that's what concerns me. They might be tempted to repeat the performance. That's why I'm sending off my own account of it to *The Herald*.

Doyle and Shaw

Doyle You didn't expect a professional London performance from our poor country amateurs, did you?

Shaw There is a difference, my dear Doyle, between an amateur performance and an amateurish presentation.

Doyle There is?

Shaw There is indeed. As far as the acting was concerned, I was not too unhappy. I have seen all the parts worse done at one time or another by professional actors at first-rate London theatres – though I confess that's not saying very much these days.

Doyle The Bard is not the easiest author to play.

Shaw But they removed all the difficult bits. It wasn't *As You Like It* that we saw there in Sir Frederick Pollock's woods – it was a version with all the seriously unflattering characters cut out.

Doyle A sort of 'As You *Didn't* Like It'.

Shaw Those parts they left in virtually acted themselves, even with rank amateurs playing them. But what really made my heart sink was seeing the cottage piano on the set.

Around Waggoners Wells

Doyle A piano, in Sir Frederick's woods?

Shaw I knew that people who would put a piano outside in the forest of Arden would do anything, and the event fulfilled my worst apprehensions. Why should Amiens sing to a banging drawing-room accompaniment? Why should Silvius struggle in vain in a tunic made for a much smaller man? Why will gentlemen who would rather die than walk down Bond Street in my hat, happily wear any second-hand misfit in a Shakespeare play?

Doyle Ha!

Shaw And why must everyone wear tights? It seems impossible to persuade an amateur that he is acting unless he has tights on.

Doyle Don't you think you're being a bit hard on a local event run to raise money for charity?

Shaw It doesn't bear remembering. I went to it in the most amiable disposition, and at the end no prudent person would have trusted me with a thunderbolt.

Doyle Well they won't invite you again.

Shaw That's the only consolation I have in it.

Doyle When do we next take the platform together?

Shaw I shall be talking to the local Band of Mercy again soon, about the evils of meat eating.

Doyle I don't think you'd want me along for that.

Shaw Does Holmes eat meat?

Doyle He generally has more urgent things to do.

Shaw And now he has cheated the Reichenbach Falls, what further great exploits may we expect of him?

Doyle Nothing more strenuous than pursuing a Solitary Cyclist down the Farnham Road at the moment.

Shaw And I'll wager he has the subservient Watson do that for him anyway.

Around Waggoners Wells

> Keep to the track above the pond. In a few hundred metres you come to the site of a Broomsquire's camp.
>
> **It is the 1860s**

Scene 2 A Broomsquire is making besoms; his wife approaches the walkers

Broomsquire's Wife *(To the walkers)* Nice birch and heather besoms. New brooms to sweep your floors clean – only thruppence each.

Broomsquire Afternoon to ye, ladies and gentlemen. You've been lucky enough to meet up with Edward Moorey, broomsquire to the Royalty. I supply the Duchess of Kent – the old Queen Mother herself – with besoms.

Broomsquire's Wife Takes them all the way up to Lunnun himself he does…

Broomsquire Wouldn't trust anyone else to do it, not I – not to supply Royalty.

Broomsquire's Wife Sometimes he sells the horse and cart when he gets there too, and has to walk back.

Broomsquire Worth it though Ann, worth the journey. 'By Appointment,' I am – I has it written on me cart, I do.

Broomsquire's Wife So who'll buy a Royal broom? You won't get one this quality anywhere else. Quality fit for a queen it is. Cheap at twice the price.

Business ensues with the walkers, who may indeed buy brooms

Broomsquire's Wife Bless you sir, madam.

(The walkers then move on)

Hunter In my time, there were broomsquires' families living all around these parts.

> Continue along the footpath – halfway along the second pond we see a group of Commoners blocking our path
>
> **We are now in the 1640s**

Around Waggoners Wells

Scene 3 The Hooke demonstrations

Commoner 1 *(To Hunter)* You wouldn't be Mr Henry Hooke, by any chance would you?

Hunter I? No, sir.

Commoner 2 Well, that's just as well for you then.

Commoner 3 He's got a lot of questions to answer.

Hunter I confess I am unfamiliar with the name. Hooke, did you say?

Commoner 1 Aye, Hooke. You've not heard of him? Why he's the lord of the manor here.

Commoner 2 Lord of the Manor of Bramshott.

Commoner 3 And he thinks he can do anything he likes, apparently.

Hunter You have a complaint against him?

Commoner 1 Complaint? I should say so!

Commoner 2 We have commoners rights here. D'you know what that means?

Hunter Freehold tenants of the manor are entitled, among other things, to common rights of pasture, of turbary, and of estovers.

Commoner 3 *(Surprised)* You *do* know! *(Suspiciously)* Are you sure you're not one of Hooke's men?

Hunter I assure you I am not, sir.

Commoner 1 *(Pointing at the lake)* Well, what d'you think of these then?

Hunter The lakes?

Commoner 1 Aye, the new lakes.

Hunter New lakes?

Commoner 2 New, yes. Hooke had them built.

Commoner 3 We hear tell he wants to build a new iron works here.

Commoner 1 He's already got one down in the next valley, down at Hewshott. Now he comes and dams our stream to form these dammed lakes and ruin our living.

Around Waggoners Wells

Hunter Without any consultation?

Commoner 2 He doesn't know the meaning of the word.

Commoner 3 He'll learn though. We've got the law of the land on our side.

Hunter I believe you have.

Commoner 1 We may not be able to get rid of the lakes now they're here...

Commoner 2 We may not want to...

Commoner 3 So long as we're allowed to fish in them...

Commoner 1 But we're going to fight tooth and nail to see he doesn't put an ironworks here.

Hunter Then I wish you good fortune. I am sure future generations will be grateful to you.

Continue along this side of both the Second and Third ponds. On the bridge over the stream there is a deputation of familiar faces.

The year is some time in the 1700s

Scene 4 Dispute between Bramshott and Ludshott manors

Hunter Now haven't I seen these people somewhere before?

Commoner 1 I hope you're not thinking of coming over here.

Commoner 2 It's Ludshott Manor this side of the water – you're not welcome here.

Commoner 3 You can stay where you are on your own ground.

Commoner 4 Keep your cattle off our pasture.

Hunter I think there's some misunderstanding – he haven't got any cattle.

Commoner 1 No but you will have. I know you Bramshott Manor lot – you'll be over here and all our pasture will be taken.

Commoner 2 Not to mention those trees you felled last year.

Commoner 3 We got the blame for that from our Lord of the Manor too – but it wasn't us as felled them.

Around Waggoners Wells

Commoner 4 No, it was you lot.

Commoner 1 Up before the Court we were, for that.

Hunter *(To the audience)* We seem to have got involved in a dispute between the two manors here: Bramshott Manor on this side of the water and Ludshott Manor on the other. There always were quarrels of one sort or another going on between them.

Commoner 2 We can see you plotting.

Commoner 3 Always think you're better'n us in Ludshott, don't you. Well show you.

Commoner 4 Come on down here if you want a good soaking.

Angry commoners

Hunter Gentlemen, we are not from Bramshott Manor – we are visitors here.

Commoner 1 Visitors? What be they then?

Commoner 2 Nobody with any sense visits Ludshott.

Commoner 3 What's there to visit here?

Commoner 4 Makes no sense to me.

Hunter We are here to visit the wishing well.

Commoner 1 Wishing well? What wishing well? Are you all right in the head?

Commoner 2 No good wishing for anything here – the Lord of the Manor takes it all.

Commoner 3 You're not friends of his, are you? – the Lord of the Manor?

Hunter No – not yet we're not.

Commoner 4 Well take my advice and stay well away from Lords of the Manor, whoever they may be. They're all a bad lot.

Commoner 1 Aye, all of them.

Hunter If you say so.

Commoner 2 We do say so.

Around Waggoners Wells

Commoner 3 Where is it you say you're going?

Hunter To the wishing well.

Commoner 3 That's what I thought. Funny fellow!

Commoner 4 Let's leave them be – I reckon they're as nutty as a hazel tree.

Commoner 1 Go on then – go and see your wishing well.

Commoner 2 But if we see you bringing any cattle over...

Commoner 3 ...or bringing any timber back...

Commoner 4 We'll be waiting for you.

Hunter Thank you for your hospitality. *(To the audience)* I think we may safely pass now.

Cross the bridge and turn right to the Wishing Well.
We are now in the 1920s

Scene 5 We meet Flora Thompson

Hunter Forgive me if I am mistaken, madam, but are you not postmistress at Grayshott?

Flora Why, good heavens, sir – I <u>was</u> at Grayshott twenty years ago, but I am now at the post office in Liphook. You have a long memory.

Hunter I thought I recognised the face. Miss Timms, is it not? Sir Robert Hunter of Haslemere – I was legal adviser to the Postmaster-General at the time.

Flora Thompson meets Sir Robert

Flora It was Timms in those days, but I have since been married. I am now Mrs Thompson, Flora Thompson. I have just been looking at the Wishing Well – when I worked in Grayshott it was a just deep sandy basin and people used to drop pins in to make their wish. I dropped quite a number in myself.

Hunter Did your wishes come true?

Around Waggoners Wells

Flora I'm afraid not – at least, not yet.

Hunter If I recall correctly, you were known then for your love of walking – and I see you still do so today.

Flora This is one of my favourite walks – through Bramshott and along beside these ponds. Occasionally I walk on to Grayshott, but I find few people remember me there now.

Hunter You used to serve Conan Doyle at the post office there, did you not?

Flora He and Mr Bernard Shaw used to come in. I confess I listened eagerly to their conversation, but I could never bring myself to speak to them.

Hunter I'm sure they would have been delighted.

Flora But I was too shy – I was only 20 years old at the time.

Hunter You are making some notes as you walk, I see.

Flora I compile what I call my Peverel Papers. They are nothing of any great merit, I'm afraid, but these notes help me to remember what I've seen each day.

Hunter Shall we see these notes in print?

Flora They are published in a little magazine called *The Catholic Fireside* – but you may not have seen them.

Hunter I regret I have not.

Flora Well, perhaps you have not missed much – though the magazine seems to think them well liked by their readers.

Hunter I shall look out for it – and indeed for any further works you may publish. You never know, you too may one day be a famous author – a household name.

Flora Well it's nice to hear encouragement, Sir Robert. It's more than I get from my husband, I have to confess.

Hunter We must let you continue with your perambulation, Mrs Thompson.

Flora And you with yours, Sir Robert.

Around Waggoners Wells

> Continue along the path and up the hill past 'Summerden' to arrive at a clearing.
>
> ### The year is 1867

Scene 6 We meet Alfred Tennyson

Hunter I don't know if any of you believe in the luck of wishing wells, but I believe you may be in luck today. Do you see who stands over there?

Mr Tennyson, the Poet Laureate, has taken lodgings near here, at Grayshott Farm, while he looks for somewhere to build a new property. We seem to have caught him on one of his walks.

He doesn't take kindly to crowds, so will you let me walk ahead of you, and follow me at a little distance? I am not known to him, at this period in his life.

(Hunter approaches Tennyson – the walkers follow)

Hunter Good day to you. Fine weather for walking out.

Tennyson I confess I enjoy walking out in all weathers. Tell me, sir, are you by any chance familiar with the natural history of this area?

Hunter No more than by casual observation. What do you wish to know?

Tennyson We are told there are fern-owls on the commons around here. How would we recognise them?

Hunter There I may be able to help you. It is not an owl as such. It is a bird of the heath also known as the Nightjar, and makes a jarring sound as dusk falls.

Tennyson Ah, we have heard it then. I shall search for it with more interest.

Hunter I believe it is mentioned in the writings of Gilbert White of Selborne.

Tennyson The good curate. I took my boys over to Selborne only the other week. We went up and down the zig-zag path there.

Hunter Ah yes, an interesting path with a fine view from the top.

Around Waggoners Wells

Tennyson But we find Ludshott Common behind the farm and the ponds here are equal to anything Selborne has to offer. I am at peace here – most stimulating.

Hunter May we then expect to see a stanza or two about it?

Tennyson I do not normally give impromptu performances to strangers, but since you have been so good as to satisfy my curiosity in respect to the fern-owl, I hope you may allow me to indulge myself with a piece which came to me by these very ponds, as I passed a rock face and plucked out a wild flower:

> *Flower in the crannied wall,*
> *I pluck you out of the crannies,*
> *I hold you here, root and all, in my hand,*
> *Little flower – but if I could understand*
> *What you are, root and all, and all in all,*
> *I should know what God and man is.*

Hunter Amen.

Tennyson And now I shall turn for home – and look for the fern-owl tonight. Goodbye to you.

Hunter Goodbye.

Shortly, by the barrage of the third pond, we find a veteran of WW1 bivouacking. He has a lean-to of planks, a fireplace of bricks and a tinker's outfit on a converted pram. We hear him singing "When the red, red robin comes bob, bob, bobbing along" and smell food cooking.

It is the 1920s

Scene 7 World War I veteran

Hunter Now what have we here? In her book *Heatherley*, Flora Thompson tells us the following story:–

Narrator Not far from the well there was a deep dingle, closed on three sides by high sandstone cliffs. Ferns and bracken and small scrubby birches filled the greater part of it, primroses bloomed there in the spring and large moist dewberries ripened in autumn. Crowning the tall yellow cliff on one side was a row of tall pine trees. When Laura first knew it, it was a silent, sequestered spot which seldom knew a human footstep. The story went that, eighty or ninety years before, on a dark windy night a horseman who had lost his bearings in the wood had ridden over one of the cliffs and both he and his horse had been killed. The whole countryside had been searched before the broken bodies of horse and rider were found among the bushes and ferns at the bottom of the dell. From that time it had been a place of ill repute. There were people still living who said that, passing nearby on a dark windy night, they had heard the sound of galloping hoofs, and a crash, then silence.

When Laura revisited the hollow she found it had been adopted as a dwelling-place by one of the unemployed ex-Servicemen who for a few years after the 1914–1918 war were to be found living in all kinds of odd places. Some of their improvised homes were wretchedly inadequate, a saddening sight, but the occupant of this one called for no pity. He had the cliffs, steep and tall as the sides of a house, to shelter the lean-to in which he slept and the fireplace in the open which he used for his cooking, and judging by the sizzling sound and the savoury smell, he had bacon and eggs for his supper. He was singing lustily as he turned his rashers, and he looked pretty bobbish himself. A tinker's outfit on a converted perambulator proclaimed his means of living. If he had a wife or children they were not visible. Probably he had no dependants, for there was a jolly, carefree ring in his voice and his face was rosy and unlined. He was tidily dressed, quite a presentable fellow in fact.

He had probably never heard the story of the dead horseman, for the war years had wiped out many such old traditions in country places, and if he had heard it he did not appear to be a man who would, on dark windy nights, hear the soft thud of a horse's footfalls beneath the trees, followed by the heavy crash of falling bodies, then silence. Horseman and horse had ceased to exist, truly ceased to exist at last. For eighty or ninety years they had survived only in man's memory, from which they had now passed, and the place had become a stage for another scene.

Around Waggoners Wells

> By the barrage of the second pond, we find see William Cobbett on the bank above us with his horse and guide.
>
> **It is November 1822**

Scene 8   William Cobbett has a problem

Cobbett Where have you got us to now, man? This is not the road to Thursley.

Guide Pardon me, sir – you can get to Thursley this way.

Cobbett I can probably get to the moon this way if I jump high enough.

Guide Only – you said you wanted to avoid Hindhead.

Cobbett At the *Holly Bush* at Headley I gave you three shillings to direct me to Thursley. Good God, man – I said it clearly enough. Where do you think you are taking me?

Guide Around Hindhead. You said you wanted to avoid Hindhead.

Cobbett And to avoid Hindhead, I and my horse have to clamber down this impossible hill?

Guide I may have missed the path, sir. I'll find it directly.

Cobbett I have no faith in you any more. We will retrace our steps.

Guide What, go all the way back to Headley?

Cobbett No sir, up to the top of that very Hindhead, on which I had so repeatedly vowed I would not go. We will meet the turnpike there.

Guide Very well, sir – if that be your pleasure.

Cobbett It is not my pleasure, man, but you leave me little choice. I either slide down this slope on my rump or I ride over that accursed Hindhead. And you can return that three shillings to me – I can use it to pay the toll

(They turn and go away up the hill)

Around Waggoners Wells

> By the barrage of the first pond, we find a Canadian soldier.
> **The year is 1943**

Scene 9 Canadians here in World War II

Canadian Excuse me, bud.

Hunter Hello?

Canadian Can you tell me the way back to Headley Down? I seem to be lost.

Hunter And a long way from home, by the sound of it.

Canadian Sure, a long way – I'm from Manitoba. But right now I'd be pleased just to get back to my hut in Headley, before I'm posted AWOL.

Hunter *(Unsure)* AWOL? *(More confidently)* To get to Headley from here you should take one of these paths up the slope, and strike out to the west across the common.

Canadian Would that be past Superior Camp?

Hunter I have never heard of Superior Camp.

Canadian Then you're lucky – I've just been there. Too much to drink, and lost all my money at cards. Now I don't know which way's home.

Hunter Your uniform is unfamiliar to me.

Canadian Where have you been these last few years? You can't move for Canadians soldiers round here.

Hunter Canadian soldiers...

Canadian This side of the ponds – that side of the ponds – man they're all over the place. Mostly in the pubs or playing cards.

Hunter Are you here to fight a war?

Canadian Give us a war to fight, buddy, and we'll fight it. Right now we're just sitting tight on this little island waiting for something to happen.

Hunter I see.

Canadian Waiting to get at the Germans.

Hunter We are at war with the Kaiser?

Around Waggoners Wells

Canadian The Kaiser? Which history lesson did you spring from? That was the last war.

Hunter The last war? Which regiment are you?

Canadian The Fort Garry Horse – finest regiment in Canada.

Hunter Ah, you're in the cavalry then.

Canadian Cavalry? You could say cavalry, if you call a Sherman tank a horse. Hey are you nuts or something? You'll say you've never heard of Hitler next. I figure I can find my own way back without the help of people like you.

(He staggers off up the hill towards Headley)

Hunter Oh dear, time travel can be so confusing at times.

We arrive at Hunter's Stone near the head of the Top Pond.
The year is any time

An inscribed stone of Iona granite stands at the head of the top pond:—

IN GRATEFUL MEMORY
of
SIR ROBERT HUNTER
K.C.B
AND HIS LIFELONG WORK
for OPEN SPACES
WAGGENERS WELLS
WERE
PURCHASED
and DEDICATED
TO THE PUBLIC
BY HIS FRIENDS
and NEIGHBOURS
DECEMBER
1919

Hunter's stone at "Waggeners" Wells

Around Waggoners Wells

Scene 10 Sir Robert Hunter tells his tale

Hunter As you see, these ponds are dedicated to the memory of Sir Robert Hunter, and since he was a very modest and self-effacing man, it would be most out of character for him to be standing here and telling you about his own achievements. So to end with, I'll just give you a short history of the man I've been playing, and why he was so honoured.

Born in 1844, in Camberwell, he did his schooling in London and eventually took a degree at University College, London, after which he entered the legal profession.

He was appointed Honorary Solicitor to the newly formed Commons Preservation Society, and developed an enduring interest in preserving commons and rights of way for the public.

In this capacity he won many legal battles against enforced enclosures, the most popular being his saving of Epping Forest in 1874.

He seems to have been 'head-hunted' for the Post Office in 1882, and remained their legal adviser for over 30 years until his retirement (hence my comment to Flora Thompson, another employee of the Post Office). During his time there, he handled the acquisition of the private telephone companies for the state and was responsible for passing through parliament at least fifty Acts. It was for this work that he was knighted in 1894.

Despite this, and also getting married and starting a family, he still found time to keep an active interest in the Commons Preservation Society, and when they found they had a legal problem in accepting acquisitions of buildings, he was the one who drafted proposals which eventually resulted in the foundation of our present National Trust in 1895.

By this time he had moved to Haslemere, and was indeed a leading public figure there, becoming the Chairman of their first Parish Council in that same year, 1895 – a busy time for him.

He retired from the Post Office on 31st July 1913, but only lived another few months, dying of septicaemia at Haslemere on 26th November of that year at the age of 69. His wife and three daughters survived him.

Around Waggoners Wells

When Waggoners Wells was bought by public subscription in 1919, it was decided to dedicate it to Sir Robert, the local founder of the National Trust.

> We approach the ford. It is the early 19th Century

Scene 11 The road from Shottermill to Farnham

Hunter Now just here you see two tracks coming down on your right, from the direction of Haslemere. *As a matter of interest, the land between them is in Surrey, while the land on either side is in Hampshire, but that's not relevant to our story today.* These tracks, continued over the ford and up the hill where the road is now, and were a well-used route in my times between Haslemere and Frensham.

Horses, mules, pack animals, even carriages – they all used it. But in the old days, the region around here was notorious for being the haunt of robbers – the so-called 'Hindhead Gang' for one – and sometimes you used this route at your peril.

Ah – here comes someone now, and well-laden by the looks of it. On their way home from market, I should think. And do you see over there, in the wood? As nasty a load of ruffians as I've seen in a long time. I think we should stand back, keep out of the way and watch.

The gang attacks the traveller – he makes his way through the audience to escape

> We cross the footbridge and return to the car park.

I hope you have enjoyed these walks. If you have any comments, adverse or admiring, please let me know.
                              John Owen Smith

Other books from the same Publisher:—

Heatherley *by Flora Thompson*
Her lost sequel to **Lark Rise to Candleford** in which she tells of her time in Hampshire at the beginning of the 19th century after leaving 'Candleford Green.'
ISBN 978-1-873855-75-1   Retail price £7.95

The Peverel Papers *by Flora Thompson*
Nature Notes 1921–27 from the author of **Lark Rise** written while she lived in Liphook. Published here in full and in a single edition for the first time.
ISBN 978-1-873855-57-7   Retail price £19.95

Flora Thompson, the Story of the 'Lark Rise' Writer – *a biography by Gillian Lindsay*
Anyone who has enjoyed Flora Thompson's books will appreciate the opportunity to learn more about this exceptional woman.
ISBN 978-1-873855-53-9   Retail price £9.95

On the Trail of Flora Thompson *by John Owen Smith.* The author of **Lark Rise** lived for nearly 30 years 'beyond Candleford Green' in Hampshire. This book tells of the people and places she met while living locally in Grayshott and Liphook.
ISBN 978-1-873855-24-9   Retail price £7.95

Grayshott *by J.H. Smith*
The history of Grayshott from its earliest beginnings as a minor hamlet of Headley to its status as a fully independent parish flourishing on the borders of Hampshire and Surrey in the 20th century.
ISBN 978-1-873855-38 6   Retail price £7.95

The Hilltop Writers *by W.R. Trotter*
In which we meet Tennyson, Conan Doyle, Bernard Shaw and sixty-three other writers who populated the hilltops around Haslemere and Hindhead at the end of the 1890s.
ISBN 978-1-873855-31-7   Retail price £9.95

John Owen Smith, publisher:—
www.johnowensmith.co.uk/books

Other books from the same Publisher:—

 **Shottermill, its farms, Families and Mills** *by Greta Turner* Two volumes covering the history of this community in the Wey valley from its earliest days up to the start of the 20th century.
ISBN 978-1-873855-39-3   Retail price £9.95
ISBN 978-1-873855-40-9   Retail price £14.95

 **Headley's Past in Pictures** *by John Owen Smith* Three illustrated tours of Headley parish in old photographs: in the village centre and Arford; to Headley Down and beyond; and along the River Wey and its tributaries.
ISBN 978-1-873855-27-0   Retail price £7.95

 **Characters of Headley's Past** *by John Owen Smith* Personalities, groups, occupations and businesses of the past which have helped to create the Headley of today.
ISBN 978-1-873855-68-3   Retail price £7.95

 **One Monday in November** *by John Owen Smith* The Selborne & Headley 'Swing' riots of 1830, their dramatic events and their after-effects are recounted from the known facts and often contradictory reports and legends which have grown up since.
ISBN 978-1-873855-33-1   Retail price £7.95

 **All Tanked Up** *by John Owen Smith* Tells of the 'invasion' of Headley by Canadian tank regiments during WW2, told from the point of view of both Villagers and Canadians. Including details of the regiments involved.
ISBN 978-1-873855-54-6   Retail price £7.95

 **A Parcel of Gold for Edith** *by Joyce Stevens* The story of Ellen Suter, an Australian Pioneer Woman, who fled the poverty of England and set off alone, aged only 19, to live in the new colony of Victoria on the other side of the world.
ISBN 978-1-873855-36-2   Retail price £4.95

John Owen Smith, publisher:—
www.johnowensmith.co.uk/books

Other books from the same Publisher:—

Literary Surrey by Jacqueline Banerjee
Explores authors from John Evelyn and Fanny Burney to H.G. Wells and E.M. Forster. Contains suggestions for further reading and details about places to visit.
ISBN 978-1-873855-50-8   Retail price £9.95

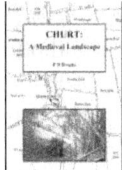
Churt: a Medieval Landscape *by P.D. Brooks*
How our ancestors lived. Philip Brooks mastered the intricacies of medieval Latin to translate and explain the contents of the Winchester Pipe Rolls.
ISBN 978-1-873855-36-2   Retail price £7.95

An Edwardian Childhood, the making of a naturalist *by Margaret Hutchinson*
The family lived near Haslemere – a life of self-sufficiency where the only machine on the farm was the children's toy steam engine.
ISBN 978-1-873855-47-8   Retail price £8.95

Walks Around Headley *by John Owen Smith*
A dozen circular walks around Headley and over the borders, with maps, illustrations and historical notes.

ISBN 978-1-873855-49-2   Retail price £6.50

Walks Through History *by John Owen Smith*
More circular walks at the West of the Weald, with maps, illustrations and historical notes.

ISBN 978-1-873855-51-5   Retail price £6.50

Walks from the Railway *by John Owen Smith*
Circular walks from stations between Guildford and Portsmouth, and linear walks to connect them, with maps, illustrations and historical notes.
ISBN 978-1-873855-55-3   Retail price £6.50

John Owen Smith, publisher:—
www.johnowensmith.co.uk/books

www.ingramcontent.com/pod-product-compliance
Lightning Source LLC
Chambersburg PA
CBHW071321040426
42444CB00009B/2060